H

Growing a Massage [illegible] ut the Stress

KATHY SCOTT

To Eve

Best Wishes

Kathy

Contents

Rubbing Shoulders with the Best: Growing a Massage Business Without the Stress

First Edition (2020)

ISBN: 978-1-912713-56-1

Published by Hands On At Work

www.handsonatwork.co.uk

Cover design: iD Creative Design

My illogical decision to become a massage therapist

"You'll have to get a job, you can't make a living out of doing massage!"

Just what I needed to hear when I was struggling to find clients and get my business off the ground—but I was determined to make it work. Why wouldn't I? Apart from the fact I had invested time and money into my course, I was not about to give it up as a bad idea.

I know it was said to me out of concern—and looking back, I had no idea how to run a business. I had never questioned my "why" (didn't even know that was a concept), I didn't know about having a vision, and business plans and networking were complete unknowns.

A question I get asked often is, "Have you always been a massage therapist?" and the answer is no. I had always worked in offices, initially in administrative jobs. Then I qualified as a legal executive and specialised in property matters working in law firms.

When I tell people this they seem surprised, but I never felt being a lawyer was really me.

I left school when I was sixteen and started a job effectively counting paperclips at the local council office. I did progress from a lowly junior clerk to the slightly less lowly clerical assistant but it wasn't long before I was thinking, "I can do more than this." I moved to a larger local authority where the meagre salary is enhanced by Outer London Weighting—I felt I had arrived! But I was still spending my days ticking off Yes/No answers and once again thinking, "I can do more than this."

A chance conversation with a local solicitor introduced me to the Chartered Institute of Legal Executives which offers an "earn while you learn" route to qualifying as a lawyer. I signed up for evening classes, and after the first year of learning landed a job in a solicitor's firm. It was my way out of dead-end admin jobs, rather than a keen desire to carve a career in law.

A few years later I remember being at a probate seminar. Scanning the room, I realised I was about 20 years younger than the average attendee. A loud-spoken man was proudly explaining how he owned the family firm, as did his father before him, and his grandfather before that.

My initial reaction was: how boring! Why didn't you go off and do something completely different? My next reaction was: what on earth am I doing here?

It wasn't all bad. I was proud at having qualified as a lawyer, I loved the interaction with clients, and the work was hugely fulfilling compared to what I had done before. I moved to a large corporate firm to do commercial work, but after a few years I felt the job had become more about, "How much can you bill this month?"—with client care coming in a poor second.

I'd had enough. I wasn't enjoying it anymore. I gave it up and a few years later found myself on a massage training course. I've never looked back.

I still don't know to this day why I chose massage; someone at some point must have mentioned it to me. It wasn't as if I used to have regular massages myself—I was one of those people who saw it as a treat. I would book myself in for a massage on my birthday and that was it.

I scanned the internet for massage courses and found one not too far away in the Cotswolds and it sounded good. My logic was “it’s pretty down there” so I signed up. I have always said it’s a good job I paid my money first before looking in detail as to what the course entailed. All that anatomy and physiology to learn—my heart dropped, as memories of failing my biology O Level 30 years previously came flooding back. I did struggle, I have to admit; but managed to get through.

I enjoyed my massage training, being with a group of like-minded people, getting to know everyone, and having all those massages every day. I enjoyed learning the techniques and even fretting over the written exams to come. Mind you, to start with, I think fright set in as this was something completely different from anything I had done before.

I know this sounds silly, but surely I must have realised the training would involve taking off my clothes in a room full of people… I am quite a shy person and a couple of days in I found myself feeling sick and had to miss a day. Looking back, I think it was probably anxiety and the realisation of what I had let myself in for. Once I got over that, I was fine.

Finding friends and family to practice on as case studies wasn’t too difficult—they eagerly lined up for free treatments. It was great fun, although I had to sack my partner as a case study after comments such as, “Don’t pull on my ears, I’m not a Dachshund, be careful of my varicose veins, don’t go near my feet I’m ticklish.” Everyone else was more appreciative. The training finished and after the exams, the massaging stops and you’re on your own. Now is the time to get serious and make a living out of it.

How scary!

Introduction
WHAT CAN I TELL YOU?

> "I wish I had known at the beginning how to run a business."

> "I wish I had looked after myself better…"

Do I know you? Maybe I do, maybe not—but if you're a massage therapist running your own business, I bet one if not both of those quotes resonate with you.

I decided to write this book as these are two common themes I hear when talking to therapists. We spend so many hours and energy on others but at the expense of our health.

I trained as a massage therapist in 2008. It was completely new to me because I had always been employed by someone else—and not in the health and wellbeing industry. After training, I was all ready to set up in business on my own—but what did I know? Loads about massage but nothing about setting up and running a business.

Our training naturally has a heavy bias toward the practice of massage, but little about how to run a business. As for self-care, I cannot remember there being enough emphasis on how to protect our own bodies whilst looking after our clients.

Over time, we mess around with marketing ideas, listening to others, imitate what they're doing, having no particular plan, and rush around cramming in as many clients as we can in case our work falls short. All this effort leads to us blending in with all our competitors, not to mention being exhausted, and all for little reward.

For at least five years I muddled along picking up ideas along the way but not knowing where I was heading. I was interested in taking chair massage into businesses but had no idea how to approach it. That idea didn't happen until much later when circumstances forced me to have a rethink, and it was only at that point I grasped any concept of how to properly run and grow a business. I'm hoping the ideas in this book will help you avoid some of the costly mistakes I made, and allow you to develop your vision for your own business, showing you how to make your brand unique and recognisable.

You may look at some of the chapters and think "that doesn't apply to me"—and that's fine. We are all individuals and some of us will struggle with certain areas more than others. This isn't a "how to run a successful complementary therapy business" textbook and it doesn't include any get rich quick fixes. I have no formal business or sales training, so this book has been written purely from my experiences along the way. I hope as you read you will think "yes, I can relate to that", or "maybe I could try that", or "I hadn't thought of that I'll give it a go."

In Chapter 9, I've summarised the main points discussed throughout the book, which should give you food for thought. I hope they'll inspire you to enthusiastically scribble down thoughts about your own business and enjoy what is a genuinely awesome job!

PART I

Discover Your Core Values and Who You Want to Work With

1

Chapter 1: Why Are You Doing This?

The coaster depicted a tiny frazzled cartoon character looking petrified peering over the edge of a huge desk piled high with files, a telephone, and the caption, "I worked hard to get this job, now what do I do?"

That was years ago when I got my first job in a solicitor's office after I passed my first year of exams. Suddenly all that theory was about to turn into a reality—and petrified was exactly how I felt.

Fast forward to the first time I opened my massage business. It might not have been files this time, but I had bought my massage couch, the oils, nice fluffy towels, and a pristine white tunic. I was all set up to invite my first clients—but did not have the foggiest idea where I was going to find them. I wasn't petrified this time, just a little lost as to where to start.

Clients Coming Out of My Ears

I had a very rose-tinted view of how things would work out when I first started my business. Firstly, one of the ladies who was a case study—my neighbour—worked at a local school and had been telling everyone about my massages. She said there was a lot of interest from her colleagues and asked for some information to hand out when I qualified. I was so excited—here was going to be my first stream of clients.

I created some basic word document leaflets on the computer to hand to my neighbour to give to her colleagues and excitedly waited for the phone calls, but I didn't receive any. Even my neighbour who had enjoyed her time as my case study didn't want to start paying for treatments. It was a big blow, and also a huge dent in my confidence. I can't remember how much I was charging, but I know it would have been on the low side to try to encourage people to book.

It was also my neighbour who had seen an advert in a shop asking for therapists to rent their therapy room. I enquired in the shop and the manager told me how busy they were. She was also a therapist and needed to pass on some of her clients, so I agreed to rent her room. I imagined lots of people coming in to make appointments, what could be better? It was a lovely room but all I can say is, everyone's perception of busy is different. I'm sure the manager didn't deliberately deceive me, but it was dead quiet—and soon after I started, she left and no clients to be seen!

Things did improve and the woman who took over as assistant manager, Alex, was also an aromatherapist. She was proactive and enthusiastic about making the therapy room work. The shop itself sold essential oils and bath products, candles, and other such luxury items, so customers had at least a passing interest in essential oils and massage. There was also a large blackboard behind the counter where each therapist took it in turns to use that board to promote their therapies and any offers.

It was a hard slog enticing in potential clients and it did feel a little demoralising at times. There was one occasion, which I can look back on now and laugh about, but at the time it wasn't at all funny. A man had visited the shop a few times looking a bit nervy, going out, and then coming back in again before eventually making an appointment for a full body massage. He was booked in with me but he didn't make it clear that he was after something more than the full body massage I offered. I tried to do the medical consultation which every new client needs to complete, but he kept trying to hurry me through it—and wasn't at all interested when I explained what a full body massage entailed.

When I returned to the room, there he was in his skimpy briefs, no towel over him, lounging on the couch in a "come and get me" type of pose. That should have set off alarm bells, but me being me and only wanting to see the best in people just told him to lie on his front and I started the back massage. When it was time for him to turn over he said, "You don't do buttocks and private parts?"

Well, I felt sick to my stomach, to be honest, and had probably turned a deep beetroot colour. I told him politely that I had explained what was involved, and reluctantly told him to turn over onto his back. After that, I just went into what I describe as mechanical mode, to finish off the massage on his arms, legs, and face. When I finished, which was at breakneck speed, I told him to get dressed, put the money on the desk, and leave. The cheeky so-and-so then asked on the way out if he could make another appointment!

I agreed to work in the shop on an ad hoc basis when they needed extra cover, which allowed me to talk to people about the treatments and take bookings. I must say at this point working in the shop has made me hugely respect those who work in retail: my feet hurt so much at the end of each day as we were not allowed to sit down on the job. It's not only about serving customers, but doing stocktaking, reaching sales targets, and knowing how to dress the shop to entice people in—and all for not much more than the minimum wage.

I was in the shop when a solicitor came in with her husband and young baby. I'd worked with her at my last full-time job a few years before. I saw her look over, then hurriedly look away again. She had to makc cyc contact eventually because I was standing behind the till and she wanted to buy something. I made a point of saying, "Hello Andrea" so she had to strike up a conversation. I get the impression she was thinking, "Poor thing, she left the law and has now ended up working in a shop." Little did she know I was enjoying what I was doing, and I was also on the verge of running a successful massage business—well, eventually anyway.

When I look back I realise now that some good solid business advice would have saved me so much time and expense. Don't get me wrong: I enjoyed working from the therapy room at the shop and in the shop itself, it was all new and exciting. But my forays into putting together leaflets, business cards, how to promote my services were all done in a very haphazard way, just clinging onto ideas from the other therapists renting the room.

All that happened was I blended in with everyone else rather than standing out and being noticed. It was only several years later, with the benefit of advice from a business mentor and from other business people I met along the way, that I learned how to seek out the clients I *wanted* to work with—and, more importantly, what I wanted from the business and why I was doing it in the first place. That all seems so fundamental now, but was a complete unknown to me back then.

Why Do You Want to Be a Massage Therapist?

I had not come across the notion of knowing your "Why?" back then. It was only ten years later, just before I started writing this book, that someone else pointed out my "Why" to me.

I was talking to a local life/business coach, The Lovely Rob[1] as he is known, about how I started the business and what I did before. He pointed out that my "Why" is to help people.

Working in the legal profession for years doing residential conveyancing, wills and probate I was helping people through the process of moving to a new house or thinking about their future and trying to make everything as smooth as possible. I enjoyed that aspect of it, knowing that I had helped them (although I wasn't so keen on the pressure of how much can you bill this month!)

Now, with therapies, I'm helping people improve their health and wellbeing. I also love the fact that through the workplace massage agency I can help other therapists get work.

How do you find out what your Why is?

This may seem mad but just step back for a moment and think about what your ideal massage world looks like and write it down. I'm always scribbling things down; I'm a bit old hat in that way as there are notebooks all over the place. If you are more up with technology then use your phone or computer to keep notes electronically. Either way, it helps to write ideas down as they come into your head.

The important things to do initially are:

1. Ask yourself why do you want to be a massage therapist?

This is not a frivolous question. Why you do what you do is the reason you get up in the morning. To enjoy it and to make it work, your business must reflect what is important to you and be central to your business plan.

2. Create a vision of what your ideal business looks like.

If everything in life is rosy, with no obstacles in the way, what does your new career in complementary therapies look like? What would you be doing in a typical day, week, month, or year? Will you be working from home, from a salon, from a hotel spa? Will you have your own salon, do home visits, or deliver on-site massage to workplaces?

3. Create a business plan.

As boring as it may sound, think about a business plan. It's not as scary as it seems and does not have to be detailed to start with (unless you're going in headfirst to ask for a bank loan or some other financial help). At this stage, think in terms of where do you see your business heading?

All three of the above steps revolve around what you value in life, which will determine your core values when it comes to your business. I remember the first time I came across the phrase "core values": my eyes glazed over, my mind went blank, I had no idea what it meant. Core values are those things in life that you hold dear. It may be that you feel honesty, kindness, and happiness are things you value highly, or efficiency, punctuality, and teamwork are important to you.

It can be difficult to pinpoint just a few values but have a go. Try to think of three to five things you value in life. For example, it may look like this:

1. Spending time with my family
2. Happiness
3. Helping others
4. Building a successful career
5. Positivity

If we take these examples, spending time with your family and building a successful career suggests that you want to be successful in your business—but you do not want to be working all the time including every evening and at weekends. So time management or working out how many hours you want to work is important to you.

Helping others is a core value we all hold dear if we work as complementary therapists. Many therapists started life in nursing in the NHS or other healthcare environments; some people had health issues themselves and discovered that massage and other complementary therapies helped them feel better, and now they want to help others feel better too.

So, What Is Your Vision?

How does your work fit around your family life, your holidays, life in general? Will you be working on your own or have a team around you—or will you be part of someone else's team?

Where do you see yourself in say five years?

Did I just write that? That's the sort of irritating question you get asked in interviews, isn't it? I used to think, "Well how the hell do I know? I don't even know what it's like to work for you yet or what opportunities there will be."

But a useful way of visualising the next five years for your own business is to break it down in stages. Will you be frantically working every hour of every day or will you be in a different phase of your business? Will other people be working for you in a non-therapist role such as admin support, accounts, or marketing?

Breaking down your goals or vision into stages was a useful exercise we did as part of a group of local businesswomen. We all met through networking and hit it off so we created what we called our Power Group and we would meet every three months to talk about our businesses and our goals.

We created our five-year plans and broke down those goals into what we would need to do in one year to work towards them and again what we would need to do in three months to work towards those one-year goals. It just seems incredibly manageable that way and achievable. It was also interesting how over time our businesses evolved and how our goals changed: nothing is set in stone.

What seems important to you now may take a back seat later on. Having a group of people, as outsiders from all different types of businesses, looking at your business from different perspectives and prepared to listen to your ideas is powerful. The accountability of telling people you are going to do something is also a great focus to act.

As time went on, we included life goals as business and life are intrinsically linked, of course. It felt a relaxed, safe, and supported environment. Is there a group of people you know who would get together in a similar set up?

How Training Fits In With Your Vision

Thinking about your vision and what type of massages you specialise in will also dictate your further training. We have to do a certain number of hours a year of ongoing training for our Continuing Professional Development (CPD). Knowing what your core values are and knowing in which direction you want to head with your therapies should steer you in the right direction.

I've been on courses that did not help me much, such as a Holistic Facial Massage course, which apart from one occasion for a friend's mother on Mother's Day, I never did again. I feel nervous about touching people's faces. I think I'm afraid I will inadvertently stick my fingers up their nose or in their eyes. I love *having* a facial massage myself, it's so relaxing—but doing them for other people? No way.

We develop our own style of working and this was very apparent when I was approached by the local Chamber of Commerce asking if I could offer some work experience to students from a local college. To be honest, I didn't want to because I couldn't see how it would work in practice and it all seemed a bit scary. But I thought about it and said yes. I could do one day for them at a client's premises to try out the workplace massage, then one of my private clients agreed to have a massage from the students at her home.

The difference here is that the students were from the local college for the blind or visually impaired, and two girls were interested in massage. I met them with their teacher at my client's workplace, which was a conference room facility downstairs and offices upstairs. We set up the massage chair in one of the meeting rooms and staff came down to have a taster massage from the two girls. Apart from guiding them to where the client was on the chair, we left the girls to do the massaging. It was interesting watching them work as they both had different styles. The feedback from everyone for both girls was fantastic.

After that, we travelled over to my private client so the girls could try out a back, neck and shoulder massage with oils. They both enjoyed the experience and it was a joy to watch them. My client was also impressed. It was evident when watching them and talking to them about what they wanted to do when they left college, that they were two different personalities and that shone through in the way they massaged.

One girl was very holistic, gentle but firm, and was interested in doing other massages such as Indian head massage. I could see her also doing aromatherapy and maybe some of the more spiritual treatments such as Reiki. They would suit her personality and the way she approached her treatments.

The other girl was more "get in there" with her elbows, lots of pressure, and going down the sports massage route. It was great.

My point is, something like a holistic facial massage course would probably enhance the first girl's massage practice no end, but could be lost on the second one. She would be better to do something like a Level 4 Sports Therapy and Injury Rehabilitation Course. If you know which area you would like to specialise in you will focus on the right areas of training.

Creating a Vision Board

No matter how pie in the sky it may seem when you first start, or even if you're many years into your business, it is a good exercise to visualise what you want your business to look like. More importantly, write it down. Or if you're a visual person, create a vision board and stick pictures on there or positive words that relate to your dreams for your business to help you plan out your road to a successful career.

If you see yourself working from premises, where will those premises be—in the town centre, in a converted barn, on a business development? How many treatment rooms are there? Do you have a reception area? Are you renting out a room or two to other therapists so the clinic offers a variety of treatments?

If so, search for images on the internet for massage clinics and print off those that evoke the atmosphere you want to create. It may be soft lighting, candles, flowers, towels, and blankets on the couch and an array of aromatherapy oils on a table. Or will it be more like a sports rehabilitation massage clinic with practical things such as muscle anatomy charts on the wall and minimal equipment in the room?

How will you make appointments for your clients? Is there a computer to check for online bookings or manual booking sheets? What does that aspect of your business look like?

Will you be actively promoting your business on social media such as Facebook, Twitter, Instagram, or LinkedIn—and what will those pages look like?

Put some images on your board even if you make them up for now. Creating a picture of your ideal surroundings and how you want to work all helps to keep a focus on you enjoying what you do and how you can achieve it.

As part of my research in writing this book I emailed therapists I've worked with to ask them for their input.

One of the therapists I talked to was Debbie. She sees her private clients in a treatment room she has set up at home and she says: "Working from home with a treatment room appears to be great but it has its challenges with children, pets and general noise. If you are working, the rest of the household has to be on board with being silent and that is not always possible. Cats in the garden are a prime example... my dogs go INSANE. If they see them every inch of the house vibrates with their craziness! Not the calming experience I had hoped to provide. They [the dogs] have also escaped the kitchen at times and as I'm massaging all I can see and hear is a shadow under the door and loud snuffling noises as they sniff across the floor trying to work out who is in the treatment room... it's a nightmare. Distracting, to say the least!"

Poor Debbie: this is just one of the trials and tribulations of working from home.

If family and leisure time are important to you and part of your core values, or you like to keep fit by taking part in challenges such as bike rides, 10 km runs, or similar, add images of these to your board too as they all form part of the whole picture.

I have to admit I've been late to the game when it comes to creating a vision for the business. In the past, I may have half-heartedly thought about where I want to be in a few years and a fleeting thought of how much I would like to earn—but that was it, there was no structure to it. It's only recently that I've been introduced to this idea of creating a vision board and realised how powerful it is to see something in front of you to keep you motivated. It's great fun to do as well.

Business Plan—Do I Have To?

One of the things therapists often lack is self-confidence, which can result in not charging a decent rate for our services.

I think the problem is because people who train in complementary therapies tend to be life's nurturers and carers. We love our jobs so much and feel it is more of a vocation than a business. This clouds our judgement because we are also business people and as such we ought to put a decent monetary value on the services we are offering. After all, how many other businesses manage to see their clients so relaxed and happy after they have visited and know they feel so much better? That is worth its weight in gold.

When I worked in the legal profession people came to see me because they had to. I am now in a profession where people come to see me because they want to.

We'll talk about charging higher rates a little later but for now, and as part of your plan, think about how much ideally you would like to earn.

Self-care is also crucial in this profession and again it is something we'll talk about later, but one thing you can do at this stage is work out realistically how many clients could you see in a week without burning yourself out? This is all part of your business plan.

How much do you want to earn on average in a week? Take a step back and break this down into:

How many clients can you see in a day?

1. Consider, if you are a mobile therapist, the travelling times getting from one appointment to another. Remember to include the time it takes to set up and take down equipment, and do consultations.
2. If you're working from home, how are your appointments going to fit around family times for meals, collecting children from school, etc.?
3. Do you want to work weekends or keep them free?
4. Do you want to work full time in the week or only do part-time hours? Just because you're working for yourself does not mean you have to work a full day five or six days a week if you don't want to.
5. Keep time free for non-appointment work as well such as accounts, marketing, emails, responding to calls, and arranging appointments.

When you've worked out how many clients you can see in

a week, divide the amount you would like to earn by the number of clients. That will tell you how much to charge per hour (obviously if you are offering treatments that are longer or shorter than an hour, adjust accordingly).

If this works out to an extortionate rate per hour at least you can see that you'll need to either rethink how much you can sensibly earn or how many clients you see. Alternatively, you may think of other ways you can earn money which is not through client appointments, for example, selling products.

How much time you spend on your business is important as there is a temptation, especially when you first start, to never say "no" to people and end up working every waking hour all week and every weekend. That may sound like a nice problem to have if you are currently struggling to find clients, but being realistic at the outset will save problems later on.

It will be tough to begin with; like any new business venture, your massage business takes time to build up. You'll need to make some decisions as to whether you do other paid work on a part-time basis to give you a source of income as you build up your clientele. Or, perhaps you'll want financial support from other sources which will allow you the breathing space to build your business without having to worry too much about paying the bills.

I had been working self-employed for a few years doing legal work on a locum basis and I kept up my Practising Certificate so I could carry on at the same time as building up my massage business. It can be a two-edged sword. It's good to have the security of some money coming in to pay the mortgage and the bills, but there does come a time when the massaging gets busier and we have to weigh up whether or not to go in feet first and give up the comfort blanket of our previous job or do the two jobs in tandem.

Don't be put off by other therapists telling you how busy they are. It can be very demoralising and make you feel as if you're getting nowhere, especially if you're still struggling to find clients. I know in those early days I did wonder if I would ever get started properly. My lovely friend, Amanda, who was on the same course as me, was working in hotel spas. She also had a great group of friends who kept her busy with appointments at home—and I do admit to feeling a little down as I wasn't doing so well at the time.

As another therapist told me, she wished she'd had a crystal ball that reassured her the business would survive, and go from strength to strength—then she would have been able to relax and not worry so much.

Running a business is never an even keel and can seem like a monumental struggle at first to get off the ground. But with a clear vision, business plan, and sheer determination you will get there.

Do not give up!

2

Chapter 2: Who Are You Looking For?

When I did mobile massage visiting clients in their homes, I took on a client I wished I'd never said yes to. He had moved up from London for a life in the country with his wife and young family, and bought an old farmhouse with acres of land.

He decided he needed a strong weekly massage—but was one of these people who thought that unless you were brutalising him and he was in agony, you weren't doing your job properly. I would have to get those thumbs and elbows in, but it went against my better judgement as I know you don't need to do it that way to get good results. At the end of the sessions, my thumbs felt as if they were broken and the pain would last for days.

He would still make another appointment, even though you could tell by his face he didn't feel bruised enough. I would dread going.

Often, I would turn up and he had completely forgotten our appointment and would be dismissive of me. Sometimes, in those situations, his wife would have a massage instead—which was a relief. I stopped going after one time I arrived to find he had gone out to play golf. I wasn't prepared to wait around for him to come back especially as he only ever had appointments on a Saturday. I was not going to waste any more of my precious weekend on him. He had no regard for anyone and no respect for me or what I did: he would not listen, he always knew best.

I will not be treated like that anymore. I value what I do, and I'll only treat people now if I feel comfortable with them and there is mutual trust and respect.

Why would you spend your precious time with a client who does not respect you or your experience and who does not listen? They are draining and can make you feel worthless if you let them. I am also certain that they do not form part of your business vision.

Now you have a clear vision of what you want your business to look like, how do you find your ideal clients?

Who Is Your Ideal Client?

Once upon a time, if anyone asked me who my ideal client was and what do they look like, I would get flummoxed. I'd say something like, "Well, everybody is my ideal client because massage benefits everyone."

Deep down I still believe massage benefits everyone—but from a marketing point of view, it pays to be more specific. This can feel a little alien, to begin with.

As I was doing mainly mobile massage initially, I called my business Bringing Massage 2U. My tag line was Every Body Deserves a Massage. I was quietly chuffed with that because it was a play on the word "body" but in some ways, looking back, it hindered my thoughts as to who is my ideal client. I didn't think about that at all. I worked on the basis that everyone was an ideal client because everybody needs a massage.

The problem with thinking everyone is your ideal client is that you end up with a scattergun approach to your networking and marketing. You spend lots of money and time on promoting your services to no one in particular because your message gets lost.

I'm sure we've all had clients similar to the one mentioned at the start of this chapter, who we would rather not see. I know that sounds horrible and unfair but unfortunately, there are people out there who do not value your expertise, do not respect what you do, or are just expecting a quick fix and believe they know best. If you don't fit with their view then, according to them, you're no good at your job. What do they know?

If you're already running your massage business think about the clients you have:

- Who do you see on a weekly, fortnightly, or monthly basis—and who just rings now and again out of the blue?
- What type of treatment do they have and how much do you charge them?

If you calculate how much you charge and how many treatments they have in a year, you can work out their average financial value to your business.

Think about the clients who bring you the most income and see if there are any common traits. Do they all have similar personalities that resonate with you, is it the same type of massage, are they of similar backgrounds, same gender, age group, etc.?

Do you like them?

This will help you think about who your ideal client is and paint a picture of them in your mind.

I know financial value isn't everything, but it is a good base on which to start thinking about who your clients are.

What Do They Look Like?

You may have heard of the phrase "client avatar". I've only recently come across this phrase but it helps to bring that ideal client to life. You give him or her a name, you describe their age range, what they do for a living, the positives and negatives in their life, and so on.

This way, they feel like a real person which encourages you to think about how your particular style or type of massage can help them and why you want to help them.

This is a client avatar I would create for a person whose lifestyle leaves them highly stressed and in need of some relaxation time to call their own—and how my massage can help them.

Meet Jodie. She is 35 years old and a full-time teacher at a local secondary school. Jodie also has two young children aged three and five years, who are a handful as most young children are. She is married to Dave who works full time at a local construction firm.

Apart from a demanding schedule at work which involves a management role in addition to teaching, Jodie needs to arrange childcare for her children with relatives and friends and a couple of days a week in nursery. This means dropping off the children in the morning, doing a day's work (which often extends well beyond school hours due to management meetings and scheduling work), and picking up the kids after school. Jodie and Dave then get tea ready for the children, spending some playtime with them before the children go to bed.

They eventually sit down for their evening meal together before watching television for an hour or two, going to bed, then starting it all over again the next morning.

Jodie is constantly physically stressed with work demands, the frantic routine, and lack of sleep, leaving her emotionally drained. Jodie would rather have more quality time with her family. She does not allow any time for her health and well-being as she always puts her family's needs first. A typical working mum.

How Can My Massage Help Jodie?

So why don't people like Jodie invest in their health?

Jodie: I don't have the time.

Therapist: I offer a mobile massage service which means I can visit you at home so you don't need to worry about finding the time to visit a salon.

Jodie: But all of my time is taken up looking after the family when I'm not at work.

Therapist: I'm flexible on hours so I can do evening appointments after the children have gone to bed if that suits you. Or weekend appointments when Dave is around to take the children out of the house for a couple of hours.

Jodie: I'm not the sort of person who can relax easily.

Therapist: Maybe you've forgotten how to relax or feel that any time spent not doing something is wasted time. Scheduling in a massage will help to calm you and give you time to concentrate on your breathing and just letting go. The physical benefits of a massage will also help relieve the tension created in your muscles due to your over-busy schedule, poor posture, and constantly trying to juggle lots of responsibilities. It may also help to alleviate your stress-related headaches.

You want your potential client to know you feel their pain. They may not know what type of massage they need, but remember you are the expert. It's easy to forget that what *you* think is common sense doesn't necessarily mean those who aren't involved in massage, or someone who hasn't had a massage before, knows what they need. Sometimes you have to tell them.

They won't know that because you do deep tissue massage or sports massage those techniques can help them with the release of tight shoulder muscles. Think about how you can word your message to specifically relate to your clients.

Sending a Clear Message

Now that I know Jodie is an ideal client for me I can address her particular lifestyle issues so she can picture herself as the person I am describing. She will think, "That's me, I need this."

We'll talk about branding in the next chapter but for now, concentrate on your message and how you'll convey the idea that you can help your clients. Imagine the text in your brochures: rather than listing all your qualifications and treatments, build a picture first of who you're talking to. Then you can set out the different types of treatments—but make them relevant. What is Indian head massage good for? (Alleviating stress-related headaches, relaxation.) What is deep tissue massage good for? (Persistent muscle aches and pains due to overuse at the gym/poor posture/office work.)

Take, for example, the person who has over-exerted at the gym and is in pain with their shoulder. Instead of your message saying:

"I am Annie Smith and I am a massage therapist qualified in deep tissue and sports massage. I have been qualified for five years and I offer a mobile service in the Colchester area. My qualifications are Level 3 Holistic Massage, Anatomy & Physiology, Indian Head Massage, Deep Tissue Massage, and Level 4 Sports Therapy Massage."

Try something along the lines of:

"If you go to the gym regularly you'll know the frustration when injury stops you working out or that persistent painful shoulder prevents you from doing your favourite exercises or disrupts your training for a forthcoming event. Having regular sports massages as part of your training regime minimises the risk of injury, ensuring you train at an optimal level and will enhance your performance with a personal and individual massage plan."

You can then describe the benefits of the sports massage and having regular sessions.

If you can get across the message that a massage is not a once-in-a-blue-moon "guilty pleasure" but rather something your client needs to look after his or her health and wellbeing on a long-term basis, you're more likely to stand out from your competitors and position yourself as an expert in your field. You'll have a better chance of securing your ideal client.

Many therapists worry that there is too much competition, particularly those who practice in a large town or city. There isn't. Get your message right and you will be noticed.

Good messaging also means you do not have to make price a competitive reason for getting work over and above other massage therapists in your area. Do not get into a price war and try to be cheaper than anyone else. What you offer is more important.

You may, of course, have more than one client avatar and it would not stop you from working with people who need a massage for different reasons—but creating a specific avatar helps you reach your preferred clients. It also means you'll concentrate on their specific issues when putting together your promotional literature.

Just one thing I will throw in here though is the Advertising Standards Association (ASA). We can wax lyrical about how we help our clients, but do be careful not to make any claims which cannot be substantiated by research. I am aware that in the past therapists have claimed to be able to cure certain conditions and diseases without being able to substantiate what they are saying. It is also wise to state somewhere that complementary therapies are just that, complementary, and are not a substitute for medical advice and assistance where appropriate.

We'll discuss markcting and advertising in the next chapter.

Where to Find Your Ideal Client

It's time to think about the best places to promote your message, and that will depend on where you are likely to find your ideal clients.

Local Community Events

Working in the shop people often came in to tell us about events they had coming up such as Ladies' Pamper Evenings or pre-school group fundraising events and would the shop like to donate something for the raffle?

We would then jump in and say we could attend to offer massage treatments such as back massages or hand and arm massages. Believe me, every time I have done one of these, therapists doing anything related to bcauty, nails, or massage are always busy. Such events are a brilliant way of getting your name out there.

I would say the same applies to physical therapies such as sports massage, osteopaths, or chiropractors. Mention that you can do a basic posture check and you will have a line of people curious to know about that sort of thing.

There was one particular pre-school group who would host ladies' evenings twice a year to raise money for their group. I would take along my massage chair and offer 10-minute back, neck and shoulder massages for £5 or 20 minutes for £10. Once I had done it a few times the following event would see my appointment sheet for the evening filled up within the first 10 minutes and with a queue after that hoping to jump in.

These events are also a good way to capture contact information and hand out promotional literature and your business cards.

Make the most of your captive audience by running a competition to win a 30-minute massage session and ask for names and email addresses in return. Make sure it's a genuine offer and that you actually pick a winner—but it also means you can contact everyone after the event to thank them for entering the competition, to say sorry you haven't won this time, but then promote your home service/clinic and ask them if they would like to continue to receive communications from you.

With GDPR[1] in force (General Data Protection Regulations—the subject of which could be a completely separate book in itself) people you contact will need to opt-in to receive information from you. You're not allowed to continue to bombard them without their permission. Hands up though, I am not an expert on GDPR so check out the regulations to make sure you comply.

These events may feel like hard work for little return but I gained some longstanding private clients as a result. It's all about making the most of opportunities and making sure you have your literature ready to give out.

And talk to people! If you don't have a string of people waiting to have a massage, start a conversation with people who walk up to your stand. Ask them if they've had massages before, is it something they would like, do they have any particular issues such as neck and shoulder pain because they do a lot of computer work/driving/ picking up the baby? Engage with them—and do not forget to hand them a leaflet.

Charity and Sporting Events

If you're looking to do sports massage, is there a local club, say, a rowing club, rugby team, football team, or running group who could do with your services? They may have a physio on board—but perhaps they could do with someone else to help them out.

Sometimes local gyms will be happy to either have a massage therapist on-site or promote you. The therapist, Natalie[2], who I go to for my massages, has her own clinic but receives referrals from her local gym because she has a reputation as an exceptional sports and rehabilitation therapist. Sports people need to get back to prime fitness as soon as possible so set out in your literature how a treatment plan will help them achieve this.

Local sporting events or charity events are also a good way to get known. Some of these may be on a volunteer basis especially charity events. I know if you're keen to increase your income the idea of doing free stuff may not appeal but sometimes, just sometimes, it pays to give something back. See it more as a promotional event than work but you do have to be careful. Many times, I have been approached about having a stand at a wellbeing event in a business environment for staff as a "good way to promote yourself" and there will be other stands there from say, the local gym offering free three-day passes, a local slimming group and maybe a couple of charities.

I have attended these in the past and offered free five-minute chair massages and been there for most of the day. I aimed to get into workplaces to offer onsite massages but the individuals coming to the stand were not the people I needed to speak to. It was good for the staff to try it out, but when I added up the time I was there and on occasion had asked another therapist on the team to be with me, and I paid them for their time too, it was a very expensive promotion.

You do have to have a balance of what you do for free and what you charge for and we will talk a little more about this when we look at self-worth and the fact that you're running a business.

Business Groups

If your ideal client is a corporate business then business networking groups will be the ideal place to talk to potential clients. As I get asked a lot about this, I deal with this separately in Chapter 4—specifically aimed at networking for business clients.

For now, we need to look at how you create a brand so that you stand out from your competition.

3

Chapter 3: Identify Yourself and Shout About It

CREATING AND PROMOTING YOUR BRAND

I was standing in the indoor market and my heart sank. We were less than 24 hours away from having a stand at our first business expo and I had arrived to collect our t-shirts from the printers. We'd chosen black t-shirts and asked for our colourful logo to be printed on the back and our first names to be printed on the front.

What we envisaged and was produced were two different things.

The logo on the back was fine, it was an array of colourful arms and hands with our name, Hands On At Work, printed underneath; but our names on the front had been printed in huge white letters across the front of the chest area.

The printers were more used to printing t-shirts for hen parties. All we were short of was a pair of fluffy bunny ears. We had no choice but to go with it as it had taken an age to get the printing done and we had no time left for them to be changed or to go elsewhere.

Thankfully, as we were offering free taster seated massages from our stand, which was a bit of a novelty and something the local business community had not come across before, we got away with it. We joked that, no, we were not on our way to a hen party—but come and have a massage while you're here. Not the introduction we ideally wanted, but I suppose it was memorable.

Needless to say, the idea of good business branding was way above my head, I hadn't even really come across it before. I would flit from one idea to another.

What was wrong with just getting some leaflets done listing the treatments and prices printed on normal weight copying paper in pale lilac with a floaty abstract flower design and which I folded by hand?

I also discovered Vistaprint and thought it was the best thing since sliced bread, ordering all sorts of things like business cards, postcards, posters, a magnetic sign for the car—you name it. Nothing wrong with any of that in principle, but I played around with different designs, photos, colours, fonts, —all saying different things. There was no consistency at all.

Standing Out From Everyone Else

I used Vistaprint for my business cards initially as they were doing 250 cards for FREE plus postage and packing. I chose a purple card with a starflower design and thought how lovely it looked.

Not long after that, I was standing in a queue in the fish and chip shop where they have a board on which local businesses pin their business cards. Lo and behold, there was someone else's business card—the same design and colour as mine, but for a landscape gardening business. How *dare* he use the same card as me?

Even when I ventured into corporate massage I didn't get it right straight away. The business was still known as Bringing Massage 2U initially and I used a photo of a man running, in a suit and tie, dark glasses, holding a briefcase but with trainers on. It was in black and white. Very arty, I thought.

I put him on some leaflets I created using a standard

Vistaprint template in a dark blue colour, with a strange motif on the front which had nothing to do with massage. I even used pink and lilac on some cards with paid-for stock images. I would look through the various designs on the Vistaprint website, find one I liked and think "I could use that" and so another order would go in. It was a branding nightmare.

The name of the business changed to Hands On At Work and I decided I needed a separate website for the corporate business. Until that point, I had used the same templated design for my private and potential corporate clients, but it did not work well.

I was working with Mel Harris, who I had met on a seated massage course. As we were both based in Worcester we decided rather than compete with each other, we'd join forces. Mel knew someone who could build a website for us so we had a meeting at her house.

Across the kitchen table, we scoured different colours and designs and decided on bright orange for the background and coloured arms and hands for the logo. I can't remember the text font, I don't think it was quite comic sans but probably something similar. We loved it: nice and bright and colourful, which suited our personalities.

What I didn't realise was the website Mel's friend's son built for us was what is called a static site so what you saw is what you got—it couldn't be changed in any way. I'm talking about the year 2010, so this was way back when. I was so happy at the time that we even *had* a website I was grateful to him for setting this up—but, as I now know, we needed something more adaptable and, dare I say it, professional.

I soon realised the colourful arms and hands were fairly commonplace and mainly used for businesses such as children's nurseries. They were also a printer's nightmare. You'd think I would have learned my lesson but no, I went back to the same printers in the market to say could we have some more T-shirts—but forget the names on the front.

This time, I was disappointed with the logo on the back. Previously the printer had meticulously cut around the template of the individual arms, hands, and fingers, but they must have mislaid that template (or conveniently could not find it) as this time they just cut one continuous line around the outside of the whole design, which means when it was transferred onto the t-shirt you could see the plastic-looking background behind the colours. Very professional!

I don't blame them, it would have taken ages to cut round every single finger.

Professional Help

We also hadn't thought about colours, so we used black t-shirts, then we wore plain white t-shirts, then moved on to purple t-shirts because they had them for sale at a reasonable price in Marks & Spencer. We also had some purple hoodies printed with no logo but just the name of the business on the back and a mobile phone number. I think at least by that stage, we had decided that we quite liked purple.

It was time to take professional advice.

We met Jane, a graphic designer, at a networking event and she offered to work with us to design a new simplified logo which would be easier for printers to replicate. Not only that, but she also took the time to talk to me about the business so we could start to think about our brand.

But Jane was a professional: how much was this going to cost me? It all seemed a bit frightening as this was still early days and we didn't exactly have work coming out of our ears.

We had a meeting and agreed on a budget so I had an idea as to how much I was looking at spending. I have learned this over the years: if it does feel a bit frightening taking on someone else's services, even if you know it's a good idea, sort out the budget first so you remove the chance of fainting when you see the final bill.

Jane took on board our concerns about the current logo and the difficulties when it came to printing, and the fact that it didn't seem to suit our business. She came up with four different designs and colours and we decided on an abstract hand design: so simple yet effective.

We had by this stage plumped for the purple t-shirts so the new logo was now in white and green against the purple. On the website, which had a white background, the white in the logo is dark blue which looked good with the green. We were so pleased with the logo we've kept it to this day and we've had many compliments on it over the years. It just felt right.

You may be thinking, "I cannot afford the services of a professional graphic designer" and I understand that. But when I think about how much I spent over the years on Vistaprint products and printing leaflets from my home printer and the ink that it used, it was probably a false economy.

Think about your branding: do you currently have a logo? If not, can you think of something you'd like? Look at other websites and get a feel for what other people are using. It doesn't have to be anything complicated; in fact, the simpler the design, the easier it will be to replicate on printed material.

What colours do you like? I always remember when we were about to take our initial massage exams saying I couldn't wait to qualify so I could buy myself a bright red tunic rather than the white ones we wore in training. I never did buy it, but I do like bright colours.

What Exactly Is Branding?

Branding is much more than just a logo. Your brand reflects your personality, what people remember about you, how you work, your values. Colours and the logo are also part of it.

We are recognised instantly by our purple t-shirts. I like to think our brand says we are "the massage people", and we bring massage and wellbeing into the workplace. It boosts employee engagement and it is fun too. Wherever we take the massage chairs, it lifts the mood and creates a buzz. It is what I call harnessing the feel-good factor.

Once you've established your colours, fonts, logo and you have a clear message, use it on everything to create that consistency. It took us a few attempts, especially with our website, but you know when it feels right.

A New Website

We replaced the static orange website for something more professional. We'd met a local IT company at networking groups and I became friendly with the lady who ran the business with her husband. She told me they designed websites. We had a meeting with their apprentice who would have the day-to-day control of the site, and supplied them with the new logo, some text, and pictures we wanted to include—then left it to them to go ahead and design our new site.

I was looking forward to this as it felt like another big step forwards. Having a professionally designed website would be much better for our brand image and attract more clients.

The day came when the new website design would be revealed. I won't lie, my first reaction was not what I wanted it to be: I was disappointed. The colours were right, the logo was there, and it was a far cry from the orange website we had before… but there seemed to be so much white space and it just didn't look how I expected.

Several months later I was talking to Jane the graphic designer about it and she said she could help us redesign the website which would be more in keeping with what I wanted. I'm happy to say our next website was brilliant.

Jane and Nick of iD Creative Design[1] listened to what we wanted and the messages we were trying to get across, and when it was complete we had the professional site I'd imagined.

I learned a few lessons and I made some expensive mistakes. It pays to find someone who's on the same wavelength as you and who listens and works with you. Previously, I just supplied the text and photos and the designers came back with their ideas rather than working with me to create what I wanted to achieve.

We have had one more change to the website which again iD Creative Design helped us with. We had grown as a company and evolved providing other services in addition to the workplace massage. We were also doing event massage and the team had grown enormously.

Another thing that seems to permeate any conversations I have with people about the business is fun. That word comes up all the time and it's true, I do like the fact that massage brings happiness to people, and especially with the workplace massage and event massage, we have fun bringing that to people and seeing their reactions afterward. This element is also reflected not only in what we do but with the branding and design on our website.

I wanted us to stand out from our competitors and although I appreciate the business message is the same I wanted the site to reflect the fun aspect of what we do and how it makes people happy. I wanted it to be brighter and colourful but still get the business message across. It does and I am exceedingly happy.

Facebook v Website

With Facebook business pages available why pay for a website? All I can say is we receive many enquiries through our website contact page and particularly since we've had our current site up and running, the enquiries multiplied beyond recognition.

Having a professional site built and designed has been well worth it and outweighs the cost.

From a personal point of view, if I'm searching for a therapist to join the team, I look up the professional directories. The first thing I look for is a website address as they usually have an "About Us" page and you can glean so much about a person from this. It wouldn't put me off contacting someone if they don't have a website, but it is certainly the first thing I look for.

I suppose it depends on who you want to attract. If your clients or potential clients are likely to use social media rather than search websites then a Facebook business page is a good alternative. You can use it as a website by posting blogs or articles, useful hints, advice, and tips or invite people to make appointments. Keeping it current is the most important thing; there's nothing worse than landing on a Facebook page to find the last post was made four years ago.

How To Promote Your New Brand

Time to get your brand out into the public domain: we need to promote you on various offline and online platforms. Let's start with online first.

Social Media

Do you post much on Facebook, LinkedIn, Instagram, or Twitter? I always felt I was playing with it. I knew it could be useful but I could never think what to say, and finding the time was another issue.

What would I have to say that people would be interested in? How often should I post? What good would it do?

I felt like this for ages, torn between the need to do it and not having the confidence to think anyone would find it useful.

I set up my Facebook business page, a Twitter account,

and registered on LinkedIn, and that was it. I didn't know what to do with them after that, so just warily posted something now and again. I need not have bothered as no-one was seeing my posts. I've had an Instagram account for a few years but have only just started using it.

I realised I needed help and one of the Power Group ladies suggested I had a word with a girl she works with for doing her social media posts—and what a difference that made.

Chantall[2] is freelance and specialises in business development. We discussed the outcomes I was looking for: to be more visible was the main purpose. I gave her admin rights to our various social media platforms and she started full steam ahead posting information. Initially, she would post where the team was working each day. So she might say "Karen is at Mr. Sunnyside Creative Agency in London today to provide our lovely workplace massage" or "Peter is in Birmingham at Cream Cakes Limited."

As she became more familiar with the business we had regular meetings to devise marketing ideas to put out on social media. She attends many networking events on my behalf and maintains a customer relationship system. It's often easier for someone else to sell your business, and Chantall has been worth her weight in gold.

Marketing

We were exhibiting at a Chamber of Commerce expo and I was walking around looking at the other stands. I came across a digital agency[3]. That term didn't mean much to me at the time, and I didn't think I had any need for what they offered. On their stand, they had a game—the one where you have to trace around a metal wire without touching it otherwise the buzzer goes off. Nothing to do with what they were selling but, if I remember rightly, you had to fill out contact details to take part in the game.

Their brand image is that of cowboys and cowgirls.

In the post a few days letter I received a letter from them thanking me for visiting their stand and letting me know that if I needed any help with digital marketing I could get in touch.

Inside was a tiny Lego figure of a cowboy.

How clever, because I kept that Lego cowboy on a shelf and it was a constant reminder of that company. I started following them on their social media channels and signed up to receive an email each Friday, where they share funny stories from the internet. I thought, “I like these people.”

It was a few years later before I bought from them but they stuck in my mind. When they advertised a six-week online course on everything digital marketing and at a very reasonable price, I felt I trusted them enough to buy from them. I could not have chosen better, they give such good value. I have been stalking them and occasionally buying from them ever since! Their help has shaped my approach to social media no end.

This is where consistency in your brand goes a long way to being recognised and trusted: people get used to seeing your colours, your particular graphics, or your style whether that is writing or the services you offer. It gives you the opportunity for your personality to shine through and for people to warm to you and trust you enough to buy from you.

I Have Nothing To Say

Does the idea of writing blogs fill you with fear? If the thought of not having anything interesting to say is stopping you from writing blogs or social media posts, I understand where you’re coming from. I thought like that for ages, up until only a few years ago—and even now I sometimes hear myself saying, "What are you doing, why would anyone want to know what you think or why would this be useful to anyone?"

There are loads of people out there writing about the same thing. You've got to remind yourself that you are an expert in your field, you have trained to do what you do, you are qualified in what you do, and people love what you do. Think of all the lovely comments you get from your clients, they wouldn't say those things if you didn't know your stuff and were good at it.

Blogs don't have to be full-blown essays and if you write about what you know there's no reason why you can't do it well. You could start with some simple tips and advice.

Think about what you learned on your course, say about stretches, or simple exercises people can do if their neck and shoulders are feeling a bit tight. Tell them what to do and offer a simple explanation as to why those particular stretches or exercises help.

Think about the aftercare advice you give to people after their treatment, i.e. drink plenty of water (and say why this is important) and to rest for a while (plus an explanation as to why). Already, you have a simple blog there—but it's information you've learned and know off the top of your head. Your clients don't necessarily know they need to do those things or why.

If you practice reflexology, not many people (me included as I've never trained in reflexology) know what the correlation is between the different areas on the foot to various organs in the body. You could write a blog concentrating on, say, digestive problems and which part of the foot relates to that, how reflexology can detect any issues, and then advise as to what they can do to alleviate any problems. As long as you write about what you know, what you're trained in, and don't start making wild claims to be able to heal people from incurable diseases, there is a whole heap of information at your fingertips with which you can enlighten people.

If you're a sports massage therapist, you could do a series of blogs to help your clients who may be in training for an event coming up such as a 10k run or a 100-mile cycle ride. Tell them what treatments and exercises will help their training to minimise the risk of injury.

If you've trained in Indian Head Massage, how many people apart from therapists know the explanations about chakras? Write about those, what they mean, the effect they have on our bodies, what we can do to re-balance the chakras. Many people would find that fascinating.

You may have read an article in one of the therapist journals which you found interesting. Why not refer to that and say why you found it interesting and how it could help your clients. Or, maybe you have done some additional training, write about that and the new treatments you can now offer clients.

By doing this you are associating your name and brand with helping people. This will make you stand out from the local competition and people will remember you next time they need treatment or know someone who could do with your services.

When you think about everything you learned during training and the general information out there about health and wellbeing, you'll soon start to think of things. If anything comes to mind write down the idea with pen and paper or make a note on your phone and make a list of ideas and you can go back to that list and expand on them when you are ready. You may even start to enjoy writing.

Online Directories

Although not targeting specific groups, I used the many free directories on the internet where you can list your business. Yell.com and Thomson Local were a couple but there are plenty of others out there as well. Some of them will contact you and try to upsell you to a paid listing but just be strong.

Be aware though, that some don't distinguish between the type of massage you offer and other types of massage of the sensual/erotic nature and you may receive some unwelcome calls. I remember being quite shocked at this initially, I was so naïve. I remember a man ringing me one Saturday afternoon asking if I wanted to come out to play today, others wanting to know did I offer extras, do I offer happy endings (I had no idea what that meant, and when I found out I blushed and came over all unnecessary as my Mum would have said). Others would mumble about am I working but this could be late at night or indeed the early hours of the morning. One man must have been desperate for my services as he rang me initially, it came up as a missed call, a few minutes later, he left a voicemail, and about five minutes after that he sent me a text and this was around 3 am. I presume he sorted himself out in the end.

I soon learned to turn off my phone at night. The shock turned into anger and now I just shrug it off with an under-the-breath "how pathetic."

Just on the subject of men, I do have some sympathy with those who genuinely are looking for a remedial massage rather than the "happy ending" because unless someone is recommended to them, how do they know where to go? It's not too bad if they're looking for a sports massage because most sports therapists make this clear in their advertising—but there are men out there who don't necessarily want a sports massage.

There is also the reluctance of many female therapists accepting new male clients unless they're related to, or friends with, an existing female client—which is understandable from a safety aspect. Over the years, apart from that one male in the therapy room, I amassed quite a few regular male clients who were all lovely.

Facebook

Facebook is an obvious platform on which to promote your business particularly if you don't want to create a website. It is advisable to have a separate business page to your personal one so you concentrate on promoting offers, information, and advice on the business page and leave the personal posts on your other page.

Just like your personal profile, a business page is free. You can, of course, share anything you want from the business page to your personal page.

I am not a social media guru. I know there are loads of things you can do with your business page to promote your services, create a community, use it to promote your business, post videos, photos, blogs or pay for Facebook adverts. I would strongly recommend you find an expert to advise you on how to get the most out of your page or look online for video tutorials.

Reviews And Testimonials

Nothing can beat word of mouth for referrals and I'm sure your clients are more than happy to do this.

The best time to ask them is when they have just had a massage and feel fabulous. Give them some of your business cards or leaflets to hand out to their friends too.

Another way is to ask them to leave a review either on one of the directory sites or your Facebook page.

Forums

Good places to have your details are on "Find A Therapist" pages of the several therapy professional associations. Embody For You[4] is the Complementary Therapists Association[5] (CThA) directory, the Federation of Holistics Therapy[6] (FHT) is another.

You may belong to another professional body, see if they too have a directory of therapists. These will all come up in search results. But a plea from me, do make sure your contact details are clear. These are some of the first places I look if I'm sourcing therapists to join the team in a particular area and it is so frustrating if there's limited information about the therapist—for example, no email address and/or phone number. What's the point? We know your name, we know the type of treatments you do, but we don't know how to contact you.

There are also specific therapy directories where you can list your details such as the Therapy Directory [7]or Natural Therapy Pages[8] but they may be subject to a small registration fee. They're worth looking at but keep an eye on how many enquiries you receive through those pages to see if you're covering your fees.

Advertising

The important thing is to make yourself visible in your local area. Look for community pages for your town or county and see which groups could be good contacts for you. These may take the shape of local directories posted through the door or online groups. For example, there may be exercise classes or yoga classes you could either join or if you didn't want to you could still have a word with the class instructor about your massage and see if there was any opportunity to do some mini massages after a class or do a talk for them about the benefits of massage after exercise.

It might be worth approaching the editor of any local magazines, online or hard copy, to see if they would publish an article by you giving some simple advice and tips as to the importance of massage, for example, after exercise at the gym or the importance of stretching or a few simple self-massage techniques. They may well want you to place an advert too immediately underneath or to the side of the editorial.

Is paid advertising worth it?

I've had mixed success over the years. There was a local magazine distributed free to properties in certain postcode areas and I ran an advert in there for my mobile massage and I always knew when the magazine was available because I would receive a phone call from someone wanting a massage. The cost of the advert was the equivalent of one massage session so as long as I acquired at least one new client per month it was worth it. I stopped advertising in the end as I couldn't take on any more new clients. On the other hand, I have been stung with expensive advertising for corporate work.

When I turned my focus to doing workplace massage I took on a short term tenancy in a business park. Now I don't know if as soon as a new business takes on a rental in the building they immediately let the sales representative know but a glossy lifestyle magazine appeared in the office together with a meeting arranged to discuss putting in an advert.

Sales representatives are in their job because they are good at convincing you that as the magazine is distributed to so many thousands of businesses, hotels, restaurants, and shops in the area it will be a fantastic opportunity for you to get known, and apparently, they are all your target audience. A quarter-page would be good, every month, so they said. Well, needless to say, we didn't get any response to those adverts, and eventually, I said I wouldn't be advertising anymore. Blow me if I didn't make the same mistake again a few more times, a national charity magazine was one and a sports club diary was another. They are good salespeople!

As a result, I've always said that paid advertising doesn't

work. In hindsight, this all happened in the early days when I didn't have any idea as to who my ideal client looked like and I also didn't have a clear message. Perhaps I just wasn't getting the message across in the right way as to the benefits of what we had to offer.

All I would say is be careful if approached to do this kind of advertising. There probably are more cost-effective ways of getting known but different approaches work for different people.

Girls On Film

When I had a few clients under my belt and the first professional website was in progress, I decided to investigate having a short corporate video made to showcase what we did. It was also about the time our local authority was offering Business Booster Grants to help small businesses grow their business. If you had a specific project you needed assistance with you could apply for a grant up to a certain level and they would match the funding required.

Periodically, various business grants become available and it is worth checking with your local Chambers of Commerce or local authority to seek out help available to local businesses. Remember, grants are different from loans, grants do not need to be repaid.

Loans are another source of raising finance and again your local Chamber of Commerce may be able to point you in the direction of trusted companies who specifically help small businesses. You will need to budget for repayments if you do go down this route.

I completed the Booster Grant application and needed three quotes from corporate video producers. I asked people I'd met at networking for recommendations. They all came back with completely different levels of quotes and I just didn't know who to go with. As it happened, I was at a networking event soon after and ended up sitting next to one of the guys, Mick Foley[9], who had given me a quote. We got chatting and he told me about how he would do the filming and editing and what was involved and I thought, "I could work with you." He proposed putting captions to the film with a music background, so no having to talk to the camera which pleased me. His quote was much higher than the other two but I felt I could trust him to do a good job and would feel comfortable working with him.

I put my application in for the grant. The amount offered was not as much as I had hoped but still a great help and the filming began. Mick filmed Mel and me over two days at a conference room venue, two of our clients' offices, and even a dog boarding/therapy business. I have to say the dog in the hydrotherapy pool shaking his wet fur all over Mel as she was massaging was probably the highlight of the film. It was great fun to do.

What was also clever is the way our simplified "hand" image from our logo was animated throughout the film. We visited Mick's place for the viewing over cups of tea and cheese and pickle sandwiches provided by his mum—what could be better? The film was added to our new website and I used the video link in the footer of emails to send to potential clients so they could see the seated massage in action. It's useful to have and I would recommend it to anyone as a good promotional tool.

You now have your branding sorted and it's time to step outside your front door and meet people. Let everyone know who you are.

4

Chapter 4: You Mean I Have To Talk To People?

Staring in the mirror in the ladies cloakroom I'm talking to myself saying, "Deep breaths now, you can do this, you can do this"—but I'm not convincing myself. I'm about to walk into a room full of people I don't know and I'm scared. What if everyone turns round and looks at me and then turns away again, you know, the equivalent where in films someone walks into a bar, the music stops and everyone stares?

What do I do first?

How can I start up a conversation with someone when they're already talking to other people—I can't just butt in, that's rude.

My fears are compounded as I walk closer to the room. I can hear the room is full of chatter, only just louder than my heart which is pounding nineteen to the dozen in my chest.

This feeling of dread of walking into a crowded room is more common than we realise. So why, if we're all in the same boat, do we feel so nervous about networking? We all think everyone else is more confident than us, that they are more successful than we are, they won't be interested in what we do.

In other words, we've already convinced ourselves before we walk through the door that it's going to be a waste of time.

Some of this is a lack of self-confidence, from which many people suffer, including those already in that room. But also because we judge a situation before giving it a chance. I have been guilty of that in the past and sometimes still find myself doing this, where I've entered a networking group and looking around the room I see what I perceive to be loads of grey men in grey suits and immediately think, "Well, not worth talking to them as they won't want the services I offer."

Taking a situation on face value can lead to you missing out on potential work.

I'm Not a Natural Salesperson

So, where do you start? Where do you go?

It would be useful here to keep in mind your client avatar as some environments are going to be more useful than others. But what if you're no good at being a salesperson, how are you going to get people to buy from you?

I am quite introverted and I have annoyed myself immensely over the years knowing it has held me back. You often hear people say they could sell anyone else's business quite easily but can't do the same for themselves, and I am the same. Also, you hear (and I have said this too) that I am not a salesperson, so I find it difficult to ask people to buy my services.

These are valid points and more common than you may think. But if you start thinking about the service you offer people and the benefits it will give them, and how much better they'll feel if they start having massages from you, it's easier to think about it as a conversation rather than a sales pitch. If you think of it as selling, then price also becomes a major thing in your mind—and how are you going to convince someone to pay you £x amount for your service? If people are interested in what you do, the price will not be their main concern, so don't make it yours.

Forget about selling for a moment.

If you were in a social situation just chatting with friends or perhaps in a pub with some people you don't know so well and they asked you what you do for a living, how would you describe it? Would you just say, "I'm a massage therapist. I've got a treatment room set up at home to see clients/I've got a massage couch which I take round to clients' homes to give them a treatment." Or would you expand that and ask the person you are talking to if they have ever had a massage?

If not, ask them why that is. Is it because they don't like the idea of being touched by a stranger? Do they see it as a luxury? Is it just for women?

If they have had massages in the past, was it a once in a blue moon treat, or do they recognise the benefit of having the massages regularly? Where have they been for their massages, do they go to a local hotel spa? How would they feel about having a massage at home, would it work or would family or pets get in the way?

You glean loads of information just by talking to people and if you can easily do that in a pub why can't you do that in a networking environment?

I wouldn't necessarily fire all those questions at someone at the same time, you don't want it to turn into an interrogation—but it's good to find out what their objections may be to massage so you can have an answer for it. This is why having a clear message is important before you go out there and talk to people.

The best way to find clients is for people to know and trust you. Networking is just having conversations, ask the person you're talking to what they are interested in, why are they at this event, do they know anyone else there? Just talk, don't think about being there to get sales or new clients. Be prepared, of course, so if people ask what you do you can tell them and give them your business card or leaflet if they request it.

No-one likes a hard sell so don't do it, it's not necessary. Don't do what I used to do either though, and effectively be so shy that I was doing the equivalent of standing against a wall looking as if I was about to shot by a firing squad. I gave out signals saying don't come near me I won't know what to do! Just be you. If you're a quiet person, don't worry about it, there are more nice people out there than horrible ones! I'm sure your passion and enthusiasm for what you do will shine through.

What if no-one is interested?

There will always be people who either do not need what you do or are not interested and that's fine. You will not need, or be interested in, some of the other people's services in the room but don't dismiss people out of hand.

Only recently, at a networking group I go to on a fairly regular basis I got chatting to an older gentleman who I had seen there many times but had not spoken to before. It was over coffee before the formalities of the meeting started and we got onto the subject of holidays. We found we had a mutual love for the West Country and in particular South Devon. Before long he was showing me photos on his phone of some lovely Devon scenery and we had a great chat. Before that, I would not have thought he would even want to speak with me.

On another occasion at another group which is held once a month in a garden centre restaurant, the meeting had finished and I was just browsing in the wildlife section. A gentleman who attends the meeting came up to me and started chatting on his way out. He said he was going to have a look at their greetings cards because they usually have some humorous ones. We then started talking about another company that does funny and sometimes downright rude cards and it turns out he loves them too and on more than one occasion has bought cards like that much to the disgust of his adult children. Before that, I would never have put him down as someone who would like that type of humour. Just shows taking people at face value can sometimes be wrong so give them a chance to like you and want to chat.

Women's Networking Groups

Male therapists reading this, just look away for a moment. A good way to start networking is to search on Google for local women's business networking groups. I'm not being sexist when I say that; they may feel more welcoming and a captive audience to begin with. I'm not saying men wouldn't be potential clients but if you are new to networking these women's groups would be a good place to start and just slightly less daunting. These are good places for both business-to-customer or business-to-business so good if you're looking for private clients or business clients.

Male readers welcome back! Some ladies' networking groups could be useful for you too. I have been to Women's Business Forums where there are male attendees so it is always worth asking the question if you can attend, all groups will have different views on this. It may be that if their rules are women-only that you could still attend as a speaker to talk about the benefits of massage (that goes for women too!)

Be Memorable

Being a massage therapist, you will also have the advantage of probably being the only person in the room who does what you do which means you'll be more memorable! When I first started doing business networking there was no-one else in the room involved in health and wellbeing, so even if people didn't remember my name, if they saw me again at another event, they would say, "Oh, you're the massage lady."

As time has passed and businesses are becoming savvier about the importance of wellbeing, people in the health industry are popping up such as physiotherapists, hypnotherapists, and mindfulness teachers but still not that many concerning massage apart from some sports massage therapists. It's crazy because as soon as you tell someone what you do, they nearly always have some tale to tell of an injury or longstanding back pain and quite often will ask for your business card, so they are good places to attend for all types of healthcare therapists.

When I decided to focus on corporate massage I joined the local Chamber of Commerce[1] attending their events. We had a good rapport with the girls in the membership and events teams who were supportive and they asked us if we would like to do a presentation and take our chairs along to a Women's Business Forum being held at a local film and video production company. It was such a great atmosphere, the room was set up to look like an awards ceremony evening and we did our presentation and demonstration of the chair massage on the stage. When the event finished, the owner of the film company asked if we would take our chairs along to a company away day they were having in a few weeks. The idea was to set up a chill out zone as part of activities for the day.

A word of warning here, listen to what people tell you. On the day, I arranged with Mel to meet at my house and we would drive over in one car as their premises were only 20 minutes away. We were all relaxed about it but for some reason, I decided to just double-check the email for the address. I stared in disbelief when I realised we were not going to the premises where we did the presentation, but a completely different location which was more like 40 minutes away with the wind behind you—and this was only about 50 minutes before we were due to be there. Frantic phone calls to Mel followed to get herself over here now.

This was also before phones were sophisticated enough to

have maps on them. We had never been there before, it was at the company director's house and in a village in what seemed like the middle of nowhere. With five minutes to go, the client was phoning to ask where we were. We screeched into the drive two minutes before the event started and were just getting the chairs sorted when the first group arrived.

After the heart rate came back down to normal it was a fantastic afternoon: the sun was shining, the scenery around was stunning and everyone had a great time.

Which are the Best Networking Groups?

With business networking, where do you go, what groups would be good for you, are they expensive and how do you approach them if you are looking to take your massage into the corporate world?

What follows is just my personal opinion and what works for me, so it doesn't mean other groups won't work for you. If you Google networking groups for your area, various groups should be listed and I've no doubt some virtual groups too as I am writing this when we were (being optimistic here that by the time this is published we will be out the other end) in the middle of the Coronavirus pandemic.

My first foray into business networking was a women's networking group where I took my chair to do some demonstrations. That was, and still is, a friendly women-only networking group consisting of a mixture of ladies who either work for themselves (PR, cake makers, HR professionals, fitness trainers, marketers, Virtual PA's and many more) or work for local businesses such as insurance, solicitors, banks, manufacturing, IT and they meet once every few months either at lunchtimes or early evenings. I would still say that type of group is good for both potential private clients and business clients as often they would take my details saying that their husbands/partners could also do with a good massage.

Many networking groups meet for breakfast and depending on which ones you go to they'll usually start anytime between 6.45 am to 8 am for a couple of hours. Some can be quite structured and have an itinerary to stick to and may include a 40 or 60-second slot where everyone in the room stands up and says who they are, what they do, and the type of client they are looking for.

Does that sound scary? It can be, or at least the thought of it is. The times I have been driving to a meeting in the car and I'm saying out loud my 60-second pitch trying to get it perfect! And then, in the room as they are going around the table, my heart starts thumping louder as it gets nearer to being my turn, because I am so obsessed about what I'm going to say, I'm not listening properly to those who are already doing their pitches!

That Dreaded 60-Second Pitch

Let's just talk for a moment about doing a 60-second slot and how to get the most out of it. The first thing is to be prepared, which sounds a bit obvious, but there have been times when I haven't thought it through and that's when the nerves kick in.

Think about where you're going, who's likely to be in the room, and who you're hoping to meet. I don't mean specific people necessarily, but more about the business sectors you are interested in. It may be that you want to speak to people who are involved in IT to help them with neck and shoulder pain from being hunched over a computer all day. Even if there are no IT people in the room there may well be people there who know of IT firms who could do with your services.

Being specific about who you want to meet will make people think about who they know or if they would benefit from using you themselves rather than just listening to you talk generally about what you do. You want to paint a picture so people can either imagine themselves using your services or know of someone else who would like to.

If we take IT companies as an example of your preferred client, your pitch could go along the lines of, "Good morning, I'm Annie Smith from Massage is Fab. Do you sit at a computer for hours on end and by the end of the day you feel tired and your neck is stiff and your shoulders ache? This is a common problem because as humans we are not built to sit down for hours on end. I can help reduce those aches and pains in just 15 minutes with a seated massage at your workplace and advice on how to look after your posture while sitting at your desk. I'm particularly looking for introductions into IT firms in Colchester so if you know of anyone who would benefit from de-stressing at work please let me know. I'm Annie Smith from Massage is Fab."

It's better than just saying, "I'm Annie Smith from Massage is Fab and I do onsite massage." If you can relay a story it's a good way of getting people's attention. If you have already done some onsite work talk about how you have benefitted a particular client of yours.

I remember Mick, the video filmmaker we used, doing a 60-second pitch at a networking meeting and asking specifically for introductions to equestrian centres. I've known Mick for some time and one of my clients is an equestrian centre. If he had not specifically said he wanted introductions to equestrian centres, it would never have crossed my mind to refer him to my client. As it turned out, the introduction did result in some work for him, so being specific does work.

Always finish how you started, too, with your name and the name of your business because people may not have caught it the first time. Some people say you should finish with a tag line, but I'll leave that one for you to decide. Some tag lines I've heard sound a bit cheesy—although saying that, I do remember a chiropractor saying once to refer people to him if you know of anyone whose back goes out more than they do. I thought that was quite clever.

To Pay Or Not To Pay

Then we come to the subject of money: there is free networking, there is paid networking, and there is expensive networking. Let's get the expensive networking out of the way first.

I am thinking of one organisation in particular which is nationwide. They meet weekly and usually start at 6.45 am. It's a very structured affair with various people standing up reporting on things, then they go round the table for everyone's 40-second slot. There will be a speaker and then the business cards are passed around the table and members have to say if they have brought a visitor with them, or have made a referral for someone else in that group or have a testimonial, again for someone in the group. The visitors are shuffled away to a corner of the room with one of the members who extols the virtues of joining. This is so the members can talk about member business without the visitors hearing. Does that sound like a fun way to start the day for you?

Don't get me wrong, it just wasn't my cup of tea. I'd had enough of structured business-like environments, and although they say that everyone in the room is a salesperson for your business, it seems to me that eventually, you will exhaust all the people in the room for referrals.

I always said I would spend too much time worrying about whether I have given a referral or a testimonial or could find someone to take along as a visitor—it would prevent me from concentrating on my own business. It was all just a bit too pressurised for my liking. The annual fee in my mind was also far more expensive than many other networking groups, in addition to having to pay for your breakfast each week. It does work for some people, trades, in particular, I think do well out of it, as most people know someone who needs an electrician, plumber, or car mechanic. I'm sure just a few referrals and they would get back the money they have invested in joining fees but for what I charge per job it would take me years. I'm not saying don't try it, I just found other groups were a better fit for me.

As already mentioned I joined the local Chamber of Commerce early on and attended many of their networking events. There is a fee to join the Chamber and you do pay for most of the events but it was much more reasonable and felt relaxed too. They do the 60-second pitch at most of their networking breakfasts but the more you do, the more you get used to it.

Social Networking

The ones that we found worked for us the best, were what I would call the purely social meetings which tended to be early evening after usual working hours, so around 5.30 pm or 6 pm for a couple of hours or even some lunchtime meetings.

There are no 60-second slots just pure networking with people in the room. Sometimes there is a speaker, other times there isn't. It is so relaxed and informal and yet business still gets done. At the end of the day, as we said above, networking is having conversations and building relationships with people so you get to know them and build trust.

Being a good listener is key: think if there is anyone you could introduce people to. I know in the early days, I used to think, "But I don't know anyone, so I can't refer." That doesn't matter too much but as time goes on you'll be surprised how many people you do meet and connections you make. I have met loads of people through networking, some I would class as good acquaintances, some whose services I have used for the business, and others who have also become good friends and clients.

There will always be people at networking meetings who

thrust their business cards into your hands almost before they have even introduced themselves. You don't need to do that, besides which, how do you know the person is going to be interested or in need of your services? They are usually the people who are desperate to sell—but you're not, you're there to make connections. It is better after having had a conversation with someone to give them a card if they ask you for it, or if you feel there has been a good conversation ask them if they would like a card. The exception to this is speed networking.

Speed networking is like speed dating: there are two rows of chairs and you sit facing a person. After two minutes one row gets up and moves along one chair. You have 60 seconds each to tell the person opposite you who you are, about your business and what you are looking for, and hand over your business card. When the buzzer goes, you will then have a different person opposite you and you start again.

It is frantic, it is noisy but you do get to speak to lots of people! The problem is you end up with loads of cards and if you don't look at them immediately you get home it's easy to forget who was who. If I'm interested in a business or think I can help them, I tend to either write a note on the actual business card or in a notepad quickly before the next round starts so it jogs my memory, later on, to follow them up.

Another useful thing to do at networking meetings is to ask other people if they go to other meetings and if there are any they would recommend. You can then get an idea from someone who has already been there what to expect.

Following Up Contacts

The most important thing to do is follow up on the contacts you make otherwise you've wasted two hours of your time. That may seem to fly in the face of what I've said about going to make connections and have conversations but not to hard sell. It doesn't, it means you're interested in the people you've met.

The follow up may be an email or a connection on LinkedIn saying it was great to meet you and hope that you meet again at another networking meeting, and is there anything we can help you with? If you've collected some business cards from people you feel could be potential clients, even more reason to follow up quickly after the event before they forget who you are.

I mentioned that I'm writing this in the middle of the Coronavirus lockdown period, so some networking groups have turned to virtual meetings via Zoom or other video platforms. People can still connect just not physically at a meeting venue. It's not quite the same but the advantages are that you save on commuting time to get to a venue, there are no breakfast/lunch fees, and it may be that you would not have had time to go to the meeting whereas you do now you're sitting in the comfort of your own home.

I know previously I have missed out on meetings I would loved to attend because my work meant I was in a completely different area. The disadvantage is that it is not quite so easy to talk to people unless they have breakout rooms so you're in smaller groups and you swap around. I do think even after the pandemic ceases that some groups may well decide to do a mixture of face-to-face meetings and virtual meetings so this could be the face of the future.

Overall, networking isn't something to be afraid of, it's a good opportunity to meet people. Just treat it as a good way of talking to people, finding out about them and their interests as well as their business. Don't be put off if someone isn't interested, as I say, not everyone will want or need what you do just as you may not need new double glazing or an office communication system.

Be Yourself

You need to be seen for people to get to know you and trust you. Before I took on Chantall to help me with social media, I invested in the services of a copywriter to write some blogs for me as I knew this was something I ought to be doing but didn't know where to start. I had met him at a Chamber of Commerce networking meeting where he was the speaker.

We agreed on a set fee so I could budget for his services and each month he'd send me an email with some suggested blog titles. I would choose one and he'd send me back a short blog on one of the titles I had chosen. This was uploaded to the website. We did this for a couple of years or so. It wasn't until I was asked to do a 20-minute presentation at a networking meeting that I realised I ought to be doing the blogging myself and for the following reason.

I was asked to do a presentation to a small networking group I'd been a member of for several years, so I was quite comfortable with the people there. I didn't like standing up and speaking as I hadn't done much of it. It was for a January meeting so they wanted something along the lines of the "New Year New You" theme.

As usual, I left it late before thinking about exactly what I was going to say but then I thought, that's okay, I'll just cobble together some of the blogs from the website. I plumped for something like "5 ways to keep to your New Year fitness regime." So that's what I did—but my goodness, it didn't go as planned. It wasn't supposed to be funny, the place wasn't meant to be in an uproar, but that's what happened—and in the end, I did enjoy it and went with what was happening in the room.

I started reading out what I had on my sheet which was the wording from a blog and all I could hear in my head as I was reading it was the guy's voice who had written it.

It wasn't me, the wording wasn't mine and it was only

when I was reading it out loud that I realised this. So I started saying, "Well, it says here you should do [illegible] well, I don't do that!" and everyone started laughing. The best bit was when I said, "It says here if you are doing well reward yourself, with say a new piece of gym wear—but don't do what I do and that's buy a family-sized pack of Galaxy Minstrels and eat the lot." Oh, the praise afterward, that was entertaining, you are a natural, little did they know it wasn't supposed to be like that at all. And by the way, I'm not a natural that was a one-off.

The point I'm making is that there was absolutely nothing wrong with the blogs I had been supplied with by my copywriter, they were fine—but it didn't tell people reading them what *my* views were. It wasn't my voice, so how could I expect people to get to know me enough to trust buying from me?

You may be thinking, "But you just said you took on a freelance writer to deal with your social media blogs!" Yes I did. But initially, it was to do social media posts which were telling people what we were doing, where we were, and how we could help.

I decided I needed to write some of the blogs myself and as time went on, Chantall became more involved with the business. She also became a face of the business; people knew both of us from networking. The blogs are written by both of us and do reflect the business culture and its brand.

Speaking Slots

One of the best ways for people to get to know you better and trust you as an expert is to offer to speak at networking events. If that fills with you with dread, I'm with you all the way! Even now, having done various speaking slots, I still get nervous and I always have my notes with me to refer to. As long as you don't stand there with your head down just reading from your notes verbatim it doesn't matter and it gives you something to do with your hands.

I have also used PowerPoint slides but I tend to keep them short so people are listening to what I am saying rather than reading all the information from the slides. Only use them if they add value to what you are saying. It doesn't have to be *War and Peace* either. Most speaking slots at networking events are around 20-25 minutes. If you have a massage chair you can also offer 5-10 minute taster sessions of the massages at the beginning or end of the meeting.

Give yourself enough time beforehand to prepare what you're going to say and practice in front of a mirror—or better still video yourself on your phone or computer and play it back. I tend to do this now. You can time it to make sure you have enough to say or to make sure you're not rambling on. One less thing to worry about.

Remember: you are the expert. You know more about massage than anyone else in that room.

What you talk about will depend on your audience. Take time to write down some subjects. If it is a local community group and they are interested in the different therapies you do, talk about those and their benefits. If it's a business audience talk about how self-care is important to ensure you are fit for work.

If you've already written some blogs, use that content as the basis of your presentation (or vice versa).

As long as you're confident in what you're saying and you know your subject you'll find after a minute or so, you'll be fine. My voice always waivers initially but as long as I have my notes or slides as a comfort blanket I eventually relax into it.

PART II

Stop Right There!

Value What You Do and Practice Self-Care

5

Chapter 5: Stop Being So Nice

"What do you mean? You've got qualifications for doing that?" This was said to me by a local business person during a conversation we had about my massage business and the training we do. We learn anatomy and physiology in addition to the actual physical practicalities of the massage itself. As far as she was concerned, surely it was just a case of giving someone a quick back rub—literally, her words.

You are running a business and one of the main aims of running a business is to make a profit so your hard work is rewarded and you can afford to live. The problem is because we love what we do, we sometimes find it difficult to charge what we ought to. Even after all these years, I'm still guilty of charging too little. I have improved but not to the extent that I should be. It is understandable because in many ways it does feel like a vocation and overall most of us enjoy what we do.

I've also found over the years that many therapists train because they've reaped the benefits themselves of what massage provides for various health problems. Many have a nursing background and have found it frustrating that they cannot dedicate the time they would like to each of their patients. Now they run their businesses, this is a way of making up for that—but often at the expense of wearing their business hat.

I was told once by a business mentor to "stop being so nice" and to put a value on my time. Examples of how I have put other people first, mainly clients:

- Agreeing to attend events and give massages for free because it will be a good promotion opportunity.
- 1-hour client appointments turning into at least 1.5 hours because they want to chat and I feel it is rude to say I've got to go now as I have another appointment.
- Not charging enough: taking into consideration the appointment time, consultation, setting up/down, and travel to and from the client.
- Elderly clients in particular because you may be the only non-family or non-medical person they see all day and they love your company. You can't charge them for sitting down and having a chat with them, can you?
- Agreeing to discounted rates at the behest of the potential client instead of standing firm making it my choice whether to discount or not.
- Paying other people, who help the business, their commercial rates—even though it is breaking the bank—because they deserve to be paid that amount.

The problem is being "too nice" can affect how we feel, it can make us feel dejected, overtired, and sometimes resentful of all the rushing around we do to please other people. We easily put others first at the expense of our health and we get annoyed with ourselves for doing it. I believe it's called being a people pleaser and I put it down as well, for me, being brought up with the values that you mustn't upset people.

Now, at a basic level, that's not a bad thing to have been taught—but at what cost? You also have to be true to yourself but sometimes it can prove difficult.

Value Everything You Do

We must value what we do. Massage is a skill, we have been trained to do it properly and as time goes on, we develop our skills with ongoing training each year and developing our intuitive ways of treating clients. It is not just a back rub. We have invested time and money to ensure we can safely treat the clients, being aware of conditions that would prevent you from treating and all that knowledge other people who are not trained in massage therapy do not know about. Do not forget this.

I have, on a few occasions, met other health professionals such as physiotherapists, osteopaths, chiropractors who have made it clear that they feel they are on a superior plane and dismiss what we do as something insignificant. I have to say, it has only been on a few occasions and most professionals I have met are not like that.

I do remember one business networking breakfast a few years ago where the guest speaker was a physiotherapist. She knew I was a massage therapist as we had all done our 60-second slot where you say who you are and what you do. She made a specific point on more than one occasion stressing how many years she had spent learning her skills at University, not just some short course in a matter of months—and I could see it was a dig at me. In other words, she is, in her view, medically trained and as such, I knew nothing compared with her training.

It was such a shame she couldn't accept that we all have different skill sets. I have in the past referred some of my massage clients to physios if I felt that is what they need and we have worked together to give the client the best treatment possible. A chiropractor I see for my health and wellbeing has a massage therapist who works with her at the same clinic because the treatments complement each other. This is how it should be, we all help in different ways.

When visiting business clients for the seated massages, I have been asked why do they get spasms in their back, or why do they have a shooting pain or get dizzy spells or something similar. Although I can advise them on matters such as being aware of their posture at work or overdoing it at the gym, I am always at pains to say I am not medically trained and I cannot diagnose so if they are concerned about an ongoing problem to seek medical help.

We all have our skills but also the common sense to refer elsewhere if needs be. So, don't ever feel what you do is nothing compared to people in other health and wellbeing sectors, do not be intimidated by them. We all have a service to give.

Is There a Time and Place for Freebies?

There is a time and place for doing free events, volunteering, supporting local charities but there are also times when people will try to get you to provide your services for free when you are quite within your rights to say no, I am going to charge. We have already touched on this but I feel it's worth discussing further in the context of giving added value to clients but at the same time not to be taken for a fool or disrespected.

The worst time for me, from a financial point of view, was when I was asked to attend a business in London with a health care company that was one of the few who covered workplace massage in their corporate plans. The idea was they would be there to talk to staff about their cash plans and then say the massage on offer today is also included in the benefits.

It seemed reasonable to me that we would be there to offer 5-10 minute taster sessions so staff could try it out. I also asked another therapist to be there to do the massages with me. I'm not blaming the healthcare company here as I was quite happy to work with them, but the business we were attending took it upon themselves to set out a schedule of 15-minute appointments for their staff to see both therapists for six hours. In other words, a whole day of what are full sessions. In effect, I had given them two therapists and around £500 worth of massages.

Guess what: despite assurances that they were interested and wanted to introduce the massages regularly, nothing ever came of it. I know you won't get all the work you tout for but that one was pretty galling. The healthcare company had acted in good faith as they had also been given the impression that this could be a good company for us to get into which is why they invited us along.

The hospice I volunteered at soon after I qualified had a team of complementary therapists, most of whom were volunteers. Their role was to provide treatments for the patients at the hospice and those who attended day care but did not, as far as I knew, provide treatments for the staff. After I had completed my chair massage course I volunteered to do two hours a week to give the staff 15-minute seated back, neck and shoulders massages which, needless to say, went down a storm. I would send round the email and then put my tin hat on when all the requests for slots came flying back! It was so popular and demand outstripped supply.

I had initially thought about charging them a nominal fee of say £5 but the person who I approached about providing this service told me the staff were "entitled" to complementary therapies so I never charged them. I'm not so sure that was the case as no-one seemed to know of any scheme, but I didn't feel I could go back on my word of saying I would do it for free. I'm sure they would not have minded paying £5 but in the end, I didn't question it. I'm sure anyone else in my position would have charged a fee and it would still have been popular (biting my fingernails now beating myself up about it).

There came a time when my business was becoming more successful and I found I was checking my diary and saying to potential clients I couldn't visit them on a certain day as that was when I was at the hospice. It was only then I realised that was foolish because I found myself working my diary around non-paid work.

The time had come to say I could not do the sessions anymore as it just didn't make business sense. I felt so guilty!

How to Make the Most of Volunteering at Charity Events

Charities, in general, hold various events throughout the year such as sponsored walks, bike rides, and other activities where the presence of a massage therapist or two will be a welcome sight. Some larger organisations may have an event budget and be able to pay for therapists to be there either arranging it directly with you or you attending through a massage event company and they pay you. If so, great, no problem. However, local events run by local charities will often have no budget to pay you and your services will be provided free of charge. How do you feel about that?

I don't mind giving back to the community by attending some of these events but you need to decide, when thinking about your yearly budget, how many you can afford to do for no monetary return otherwise you could find yourself doing something nearly every weekend if you're not careful and end up despising the amount of free work you are providing.

If an event attracts local people think about how you can make the most of your presence at the event. It will be good to have your literature to hand out to people whether or not they have a massage from you or be there on hand to talk to people about any issues they have.

If you are, for example, a sports massage therapist, set up the gazebo with your couch but also have a roller banner made (they are reasonably cheap to have done) inviting people to come over to chat with you about specific sporting injuries or issues they may have. Advertise on the banner you are on hand to give advice.

People may be more inclined to approach you if they know they can browse your leaflets and talk to you rather than feeling obliged to have a massage. You may not make any money on the day but if you think of something to attract people over so that they will speak with you and take some of your literature you never know, they may be future clients.

Perhaps run a competition to book a session with you and get a second one for half price or something similar. This way you capture their contact details such as a phone number or email address. Follow up those contact details to confirm if they have won the sessions or if not still send them some details about your massage practice but just remember GDPR we touched on earlier.

Is there is a way you could at least earn some money from the event at the same time as benefitting the charity? Say that there will be a charge for a 15-minute post-event massage and then a proportion of it will go to the charity. If you do this, I suggest making sure before the event you let the organisers know so they put that in their literature. Or, if you were happy to use the event to promote your business, have a charity bucket for people to make donations.

Whatever you decide to do, make sure it's because you want to attend. Don't do it if it makes you feel uncomfortable or you simply cannot afford the time to be there. Remember, there is no obligation, charities are very appreciative of support but it is your choice at the end of the day if you can help out.

Be wary though that there are people out there who do not value what you do and expect you to provide your services for free and unfortunately I have to say that I include some businesses in that description. As I say, I believe most charities do appreciate the support they receive from their volunteers and if you are attending events to provide your time to give massages, then you are a volunteer. One way, we have helped is to support local businesses to raise funds for their nominated charity. One example is a college we attend a few times a year, where the college pays us to provide one or two of our therapists to attend and deliver workplace massages for the staff. As the college pays us the staff would not normally have to pay but what they do is ask those staff having a massage to donate to their nominated charity. In this way, we get paid for delivering the massages, the College provides a well-deserved break and massage for their staff, and the charity benefits from the donations. Winners all round.

We thought this was such a good idea, we promoted the idea at networking meetings. At one of these meetings, I was talking to a girl who worked for a firm who supported a local charity and so I put the idea to her. She thought it was great but when the decision-maker contacted me for further details and I told her how it works, she was most offended. She said it sounded more like a business proposition for us rather than helping the Charity. Well, yes, it is a business proposition, as we are a business, we are not the charitable organisation here, but she had completely missed the point of how it would help them raise the funds for the charity and expected us to give our services for free.

To give her the benefit of the doubt she may just have got the wrong end of the stick but there was no way they were going to pay for massages, just didn't see the value in it at all.

Do You Charge Your Clients Enough?

How many of you have just read that heading and immediately said "No"

I have often said it is a wonder I am still in business at all. I know I should be more ruthless when it comes to charging rates but I just cannot muster the enthusiasm to do so, laid back Jack just kicks in every time. That will make everything I say now sound just a little hypocritical but it's only because I want you to get the most out of the wonderful job you do.

How much do you think you should charge per hour? Is it per hour, or is it per client? What if a client books in for a 1-hour massage, do you give them a 1-hour massage, or do you use some of those 60 minutes for a welcome chat, consultation, time for the client to undress and dress, have some water, make their next appointment and then leave, after which you need to get the room ready for the next client who is waiting at the door. Is it just an hour or more like 75 minutes or more? If so, what does that make your actual hourly rate by the time you reach the end of the day. Are you happy with that?

Looking at it from a positive angle, it will depend on how many clients you want to see in a day and how many hours you want to work. If you are happy working a 7 hour day plus a lunchbreak factored in (of course you do, more on self-care in a bit) and you only want to see 4 clients in a day, then it may not be so important to you if a 1-hour massage is, in reality, a 75 minutes timeslot because you will have plenty of downtime between clients. But if you are looking to see 5 or 6 clients in a day, those extra minutes will eat into your time and you will either not factor in breaks or work a much longer day than you would like. Apart from the fact that appointments are not the only aspect of your business. When are you going to factor in time for writing up notes for each client, checking emails, returning phone calls, doing accounts, checking social media, writing for social media, marketing, networking, and so on? Some of these may not seem important to you but even washing towels and cleaning the treatment room takes time.

If you do mobile massage you also have to factor in travelling time and setting up your couch so a 1-hour appointment can easily extend to nearly double that depending on travel time.

Elderly Client Massage

Elderly client massage is another area where we quite often give our time for free. I had a lady I visited for a 30-minute leg and foot massage, she would usually lay on her bed and I would sit on the side and massage her. But even before the massage started I would be invited in to have a sit down, did I want a cup of tea, followed by a chat about family and what I'd been up to and who she had seen. Needless to say, I was always there for at least an hour. I didn't mind but I was only charging her for the 30 minutes massage. She even used to say is this enough when she wrote out the cheque and I would just say, "oh, yes, of course, it is". What I should have done is charged her for the hour but couldn't bring myself to do it as I enjoyed going to see her.

Sometimes it is a balancing act, do you do a few of those appointments where you don't charge enough but you have others where you do charge what you should so does it matter? At the end of the day, it is what you feel comfortable with. If you resent the fact that you are there for an hour and only getting a fraction of the cost then think about increasing the fee, if you're happy to stick with it then do so.

I wasn't there but I was told of a local networking group who held a meeting where they would have a 'hot spot' for someone, who had just started on their business, to ask the people in the room about a particular issue they wanted help with. At one of these meetings was a massage therapist who had just started up but couldn't decide in which area she wanted to specialise e.g. holistic massage, pregnancy, and baby massage or elderly client but she did make it clear that she wanted to do the least amount of work for maximum money. For this reason, she decided to do elderly client work. I think if

I had been at that meeting I would have warned her that her approach would probably slip her up as she may think giving an elderly client a gentle 30-minute massage would be an easy option but she would spend much more time than she would anticipate. So far as client care is concerned it is great but if she is looking at it from a harsh business point of view it's rubbish. It's a tough one. I think if we all put on our ruthless business hats and made money the main concern then our massages would almost certainly suffer.

Unreliable Clients

There will always be clients now and again who raise our stress levels. The clients who make appointments and then don't turn up. Or, even worse, if you are mobile, you travel to their address and find they are not in. Clients who are consistently late for appointments but still expect the full hour treatment especially if it is an evening appointment which means you are over an hour later getting back home or finishing work.

I accept there will be times when someone is running late but most people will contact you if they are able. If I was running late for an appointment I would phone through to say so and also to check if there will still be time for my appointment. Even if I do get there late I would expect my appointment to be shortened accordingly (but still pay for the hour) so that it doesn't mess up the rest of the day for the therapist. I would say this is showing respect whereas just turning up late, no apologies, and expecting the full hour is very disrespectful.

I think because massage is enjoyable many people, despite all our valiant efforts to get across the message that regular sessions reap more health benefits, still see it as just a nice thing to have. They forget that it is our livelihood and that we have trained hard and invested time and money in it. They forget how it affects us financially.

A small number of our corporate clients are happy to have our workplace massage service but ask the individual members of staff to pay for their sessions and so, you are relying on headcount. Many a time, I have had a full appointment sheet only to find on the day, I receive emails from some saying they need to cancel or even worse just don't turn up. I have rung their extension numbers only to be told, oh they've gone out for lunch, or they've taken annual leave that day. I appreciate there will always be times when an unexpected meeting is arranged or something is put in their diary by someone else which prevents them from attending but it soon becomes clear that there are a few who do it on more than one occasion and it doesn't seem to bother them.

It's even worse if I have asked a member of the team to cover a session where the individuals pay. I pay the therapists on the team an hourly rate but too many times, I was left out of pocket because the amount I was paying a therapist to be there for say 4 hours was more than the amount I received due to last-minute cancellations. I started paying the therapist a set fee per head instead but even then, if the numbers were low I would feel guilty and end up paying them all of the fees and getting nothing for it myself.

Cancellation Policies

This goes back to valuing your time, should we have cancellation policies in place and if so, would you enforce it? I should have a cancellation policy in place and believe me, I have thought about it many times over the years but I have never done it. It's crazy, if I was advising anybody starting now, I would say have a cancellation policy in place. I have been stupid about this. It goes back to that people pleaser trait where you don't want to upset anyone. For crying out loud, I'm worried about upsetting people who quite blatantly have no qualms about upsetting me by not turning up for appointments or keeping me waiting without batting an eyelid. If you have a cancellation policy in place you can decide whether a person not turning up has a valid genuine reason or if it is a serial no show person in which case you have it there in place to recover your money. If they kick up a fuss and don't book in again, will you be sorry?

I am sure we all have enough lovely clients not to worry about the very few who take advantage of our good nature and mess us around and in the long run, if they don't come back just think how much extra time that will give you and far less stress.

6

Chapter 6: Who Looks After You?

SELF CARE

The pain shot across my lower back. It was so intense I stood there immediately thinking, "What have you done?" I was in agony—particularly on my left side. And the pain also shot down my left leg. But, I gathered myself together and in excruciating pain set up the bed in my client's house and continued with his treatment. I have no idea how I managed to drive home after that.

That happened to me a few years ago when I was taking my massage couch out of the car just before doing a 1.5-hour deep tissue massage.

Too many therapists give up their massage careers due to health problems way before they want to. Trying to do too much leads to exhaustion and not being aware of the strain on your body leads to joint problems, especially in hands, lower back pain, and repetitive strain injuries.

Looking After Your Physical Health

I did mainly mobile massage driving from one client to another including some clients with mobility issues. One client, in particular, had motor neurone disease. I would arrive with my portable couch but it became apparent that it was too much strain and effort for him to climb on and the couch did not have the option to adjust its height. As he liked to have a full body massage, I needed to re-think.

At home, I still had my very sturdy wooden framed couch I bought for my initial training and although it is laughingly referred to as portable it weighed a ton. The carry bag which was on wheels (well, three wheels as one had fallen off) was almost as heavy as the couch. But it was adjustable so I started using that for his treatments. It was much better for him but so much effort for me as it was cumbersome to set up in a very small area and heavy to manhandle getting it in and out of the car—but in my mind, the client's needs must come first.

The problem is I became lazy and instead of swapping that couch for my portable one for other clients I just got into the habit of leaving it in the car and so ended up using it for all my mobile appointments. Good weight training you might say but one day it did land me in trouble.

I was about to see a gentleman for a 1.5-hour deep tissue full-body massage at his home. I had a small hatchback car and to get the couch out I had to tip it at an angle before pulling it forward. As I did so, I must have twisted. That was when the pain shot across my lower back. For months afterwards, I put up with the pain and soldiered on trying to convince myself that with time it would ease. The worst times would be getting in and out of the car. I always hoped no-one had got CCTV footage because I would not have been a very good advert for what I do, hobbling out looking as if I had forgotten my walking sticks.

Eventually, I decided I needed to do something about it, and not wanting to wait for several weeks on a referral list through the GP I booked in to see a physiotherapist. She asked some questions and said it sounded like a tear to the cartilage lining of the hip joint, called the acetabulum. She said she would give me some exercises to do and if they didn't work we'd look at surgery. What!!?? Surgery at my age (a mere 40+years) I don't think so.

I had been seeing a massage therapist for my massages so I decided to increase my visits and together with the physio exercises, things eventually improved. It did make me think, how many people go ahead with joint surgery because they are not aware of alternatives? If I hadn't been a therapist I would have accepted that surgery was required and gone ahead which is frightening.

Making the Time

I know you are reading this and thinking I don't have time to have a massage myself. Really? Or is it that you are not making yourself enough of a priority to have a massage? I am a great believer that you can find time to do anything if you want to.

Do you go to the hairdresser every six weeks or so? You make time for that. It may mean juggling things around but if you had a hospital appointment you would have to make time, so make it as important as a hospital appointment. When you do go for your massage/reflexology/Reiki/any other complementary therapy that suits you, make sure you also make your next appointment before you leave. Making it a habit is key.

Giving Up Work Too Early

I have seen so many excellent therapists give up what they love to do because it has taken a physical toll on their bodies. Naturally, wrists, hands, and thumbs are the biggest culprits but also back problems and other aches and pains to the extent therapists feel they cannot carry on. It's the irony of what we do, we spend years making others feel better at the expense of our health.

Think about how you work, do you arch your back when

leaning over the couch? Do you stretch too far rather than work from the other side? Are you twisting your body? Small adjustments to the way you stand and position yourself make a huge difference.

Many training providers run CPD courses on how to work safely. Continue your professional training by attending those which improve your techniques such as advance massage or hands-free techniques encouraging you to use forearms and elbows rather than fragile thumb joints.

There is one tutor I have huge respect for and that is Darien Pritchard[1]. He is as much a stickler for how therapists use their bodies effectively and safely as he is about the techniques of the massage itself. He brings fluidity to the way you move and shows you how applying pressure, using your whole body, creates a powerful massage without having to expend so much energy. He has written a book called *Dynamic Bodyuse for Effective, Strain-Free Massage*. As he says, the only thing he forgot was a health and safety warning about lifting as the book is so heavy!

We also need to educate our clients that the "no pain no gain" idea is not always the best course of action and those massage techniques using bodyweight to support the skilful use of our arms and hands are more effective than just digging in deep with thumbs and brutalising them.

I always remember one male client who wanted a home massage for his back neck and shoulders. He worked in engineering but was more of a desk engineer than on the factory floor so his problems were mainly due to bad posture and computer work but it was his attitude I didn't like. He told me he had an ex-martial arts instructor as a massage therapist and it would hurt so much it felt good. He was used to the strength of a man doing the treatment. He beefed himself up to be so macho. I really couldn't give a stuff about that and unfortunately for him, I slipped into mechanical mode rather than providing the best treatment. As soon as the first elbow went in he winced and then shut up. That client/therapist relationship was short-lived.

I appreciate that some techniques, especially with sports massage, may result in the client feeling a little sore after treatment but you as the therapist shouldn't feel sore from giving the massage. If you take nothing else away from this book please, please, do look into courses or find books that deal with self-care for therapists. We do not need to ruin our bodies to look after other people. Effective massage is possible without having to beat someone up and ourselves in the process.

A Time for Reflection

Just take some time to reflect on your vision of what your massage business and lifestyle should look like. Did you visualise yourself looking exhausted as if you've been driven through a hedge backward, desperate for some food, desperate for some good quality sleep but slaving away one client after another? Or was it nearer to the idyllic number of clients in a day allowing for proper breaks and downtime to spend with your family or your pets, days off to relax or pursue interests and hobbies and taking holidays? Okay, the last scenario may seem a bit 1950s idyll of life in middle-class England but you know where I'm coming from.

Life is short, make the most of it, yes, most of us need to work to survive, but we've chosen a great sector to work in, we make people happy, we make them feel better, most are very appreciative of what we do for them, we are doing something that we love, we need to make the most of it too and enjoy it.

If that all sounded a bit cheesy, then I'm sorry, but it was the best way I could describe how I feel about it. Think of ways you incorporate downtime into your working life. A friend of mine is a personal trainer and I used to go to her house a couple of times a week for some sessions but she made a point of always having Wednesdays as her day off in the week. When we were working out my next batch of 10 sessions I would check my diary but immediately think, okay, I must not look on Wednesdays because she doesn't work then.

In other words, it is surprising how clients will get used to you not working on a certain day or you may want to work lesser hours on a particular day. In other words, you dictate when you are available for appointments, not the other way round, permit yourself to be in control of your diary.

Time Management

Time management is an important part of self-care because you need to make sure you are not so busy looking after everyone else's needs that you neglect your own. Running a business is not just about the appointments but everything else that goes with it such as accounts, record keeping, ordering supplies, marketing and advertising, networking, and so on. We wear so many different hats and some which to be honest we are not experts in.

One way of doing this is to think about some of the non-appointment jobs and whether you can outsource them. I had been in business about 5-7 years before I decided I could do with some help with the accounts. I had already enlisted the help of a firm of accountants before I started the massage business as I had been self-employed in a different sector. My accounts were pretty straightforward then and I could probably have done them myself but I kept thinking well, they know all the ins and outs of what allowances you could use, for example, using the house as an office.

Although I had accountants on board from day one I was still traipsing up to their offices once a year with my spreadsheets and carrier bags full of invoices and receipts. It also meant I was still spending time typing up the spreadsheets, trying to keep on top of the accounts (which I never did, it was always a mad rush at the end of the financial year) getting all the invoices and receipts together, hunting for hours looking for lost receipts and tearing my hair out.

At one of the networking groups I attended there was a bookkeeper[2] and I wondered about asking him if he could help but I was afraid it was going to cost me too much money and I wouldn't be able to afford both him and the accountants. I bit the bullet and asked if we could have a meeting. Well, I was pleasantly surprised: we talked through the business and what the average number of transactions would be per month and we agreed on a very affordable monthly fee. The main change he implemented was putting me on an accounting software system called Xero which substantially reduced my paperwork.

Running the onsite massage company meant typing out Word documents for agents to send them job confirmation sheets. I would then type out further Word documents after the jobs as remittance advices and keep them all in various folders.

With the new software, there was a job confirmation template and which over time would store information so that agents and client details would flash up automatically and at the touch of a button I could send out the jobs. It also meant that when I had paid an agent for a job the system automatically updates to show this has been paid. At a glance, I can see at any one time who owes me money and bills I need to pay.

The upshot is I no longer spend hours typing up Word documents and wasting time trying to find paperwork that I should have been keeping neatly in one place but which in practice never happened. Freeing up that time has been invaluable.

Over the years, my bookkeeper has shown me other ways how to use Xero and its app to streamline all this non-fee earning time. The accountants are probably relieved too that I no longer appear at their door under a ton weight of carrier bags stuffed with papers.

Support Groups

We touched upon making it a priority to find time to have a massage yourself, this is so important. Are there other therapists locally with whom you could swap treatments? It is always good anyway to get a massage from someone else as it not only gives you some downtime but it reminds you how good it feels to have a massage. You can also swap ideas and try out different techniques.

Support groups are also beneficial to self-care especially if you choose to work from home or mobile as opposed to working in a salon or clinic with other therapists. It can feel quite isolating otherwise.

When you think of when you train, you are surrounded by other like-minded people eager and enthusiastic to learn about massage, you have treatments several times a day as part of the learning process and the buzz from being in that situation is infectious. Then, all of a sudden, the exams are out of the way, you qualify, and you are on your own. Initially, it's fine as you are excited about setting up your treatment room and getting everything looking lovely for that long line of clients about to knock at your door but after a while, you do start to miss everyone.

When I first completed my Level 3 course the college had put us in touch with the Complementary Therapists Association (CThA) a professional body that we were encouraged to join. Upon joining I received my confirmation letter which said, unfortunately, there was no local group in my area so I thought, blow this, I'll start one and so I applied to be a local group coordinator.

After a bit of form filling, I was then the local group coordinator and given a list of therapists in my area to contact. We had a meeting at my house and the Be Inspired group was born. It wasn't long before we opened it up to all therapists in the area who were not necessarily members of the CThA as people knew others who wanted to join. I was so pleased I did that as once again I was surrounded by therapists who practiced all different types of therapies.

We organised a couple of complementary therapy days where we hired a local hall and between us advertised where we could locally to encourage members of the public to come along and try out anything from massage, Reiki, sports massage, infant massage, tarot readings, and healthcare products for sale. We also enlisted the help of friends and relatives to man the kitchen to offer tea and cake, it was great and the therapists had the opportunity to chat with each other.

We used to meet once a month to talk about local courses and issues anybody wanted to bounce off others, in other words, the support of a group of people who between them had varying levels and years of experience. This group was started in 2009. The modern-day version is the support groups you find online.

There are several therapists network groups on Facebook which are well worth joining. You learn so much from other people as well as keeping in touch with what is going on and courses available.

That was something else that came up in my research for this book: imposter syndrome. We all know the training we have done is not to be sniffed at, all that anatomy and physiology, the pathology, the health and safety exam questions and that's before we get on to the actual massaging itself and yet sometimes we question ourselves as to whether we are good enough, do we know enough.

I went through a terrible phase of this, I used to listen to other therapists talking about different things such as stretches and exercises they have recommended to their clients for specific conditions or talking about medications or illnesses or conditions I hadn't heard of before. I would be thinking to myself, how do they know all this, I don't remember that being covered in the course? That would lead to me feeling insecure and thinking that somehow I had managed to pass my exams without actually learning anything. How stupid is that?

What we should do is think, I don't know about that, where can I find out and there is no shame in asking questions, no-one is going to think you are silly as there are probably loads of other people thinking the same but are not confident enough to say anything. The online groups are good platforms for this as it is surprising, in a very good way, how eager people are to help out and offer advice and guidance.

There is a good support network out there. So, get Googling!

How Mindful Are You?

Recently, Chantall and I took part in a workplace wellness challenge run by a business based in the Midlands. It was a six-week challenge to improve our health and wellbeing at work by setting daily challenges and tasks aimed at making you think about how much exercise you get in a day, what you eat and drink, how much time you take out for just being you. It was a really good learning curve as it certainly made me realise how much time I sit down in a day.

I always thought I was on the go all the time and so reaching 10,000 steps in a day would be easy—but not so. I always said I would not be a slave to a fitness tracker but I had to invest in one to know how many steps I was taking. Some days, I had to force myself to go out for a walk to get my steps up.

But the other thing the challenge encouraged was to practice some meditation or mindfulness every day. I have always been one of those people who say I cannot meditate because my perception was that you had to clear your mind. Are you joking? No way, could I clear my mind, it's on the go all the time. I always remember seeing a picture of Kermit from The Muppets lazing on his back with his head resting on his hand (or foot, do frogs have hands?) and the caption was, "I may look as if I'm not doing anything, but in my head, I am really busy" and that sums me up.

I have learned you don't have to clear your head it is just being quiet and being aware of your surroundings. It was still a struggle though to think of finding a way to incorporate that into every day, when on earth would I have time? As part of the challenge you had to record your activity every day so I needed to find the time. And I did. Even if it was just for ten minutes I would purposefully find somewhere to go and sit and just close my eyes and concentrate on taking slow deep breaths. I can't believe I am saying that as I can be a very sceptical being but it does help.

It's surprising when you're not thinking about anything in particular what comes to mind and quite often, something I may have been struggling with, perhaps writing a blog and knowing what I want to say but not quite knowing how to express it, would suddenly come into my head. Just as an aside here, that is also one of the great things about massage, which I'm sure I don't need to tell you. I remember the one time doing the seated massage at the local hospital and a nurse came in for his massage. He is on the adult mental health team and he'd had a very stressful day dealing with two people who had suicidal thoughts. Just sitting in my massage chair for 20 minutes, in a quiet room, he was able to calm his mind and by the end of the session, he said he had worked out a plan for one of those clients.

I hear you if you say you wouldn't be able to find the time, as up to when we did that challenge, I would have said the same but it's like anything else if you make it a priority as part of your self-care plan you will find the time even if it is for only 10 minutes. My favourite distraction, and what I used to class as my mindfulness or meditation was sitting down the garden with my chickens. We just had the three of them but sitting quietly listening to them scratching around and their funny little noises were so peaceful. Quite often, if I was just sitting there quietly they would fly up on to the bench to join me, have a preen then settle down to have a doze. I was in heaven and felt awful at disturbing them when I had to get up to go back to work.

Trying to eat healthily and drinking plenty of water during the day and getting a good night's sleep is essential for keeping you fit and strong, you know, everything you advise your clients to do but you don't do yourself. I'm not about to preach about what you should and shouldn't eat, primarily because I'm not a qualified nutritionist, but we are all human and we're all adults. I'll just leave it at that, having just walked past a bowl of fruit and instead eaten a couple of chocolate biscuits.

Being Kind

Another form of self-care, I believe, is being kind to others (I'm going for the cheesy one-liners now aren't I?) but it's true. It's lovely to be able to help others and makes you feel good inside. One thing Mel and I did for a couple of years running was to take our therapies out to Bosnia with a charity called Healing Hands Network[3].

I came across their stand at a Holistic Health Show in Birmingham in 2011. They send therapists out to Bosnia between April to October each year to provide a myriad of complementary therapies to those who are suffering from the mental, physical and emotional after-effects of war and who suffer from PTSD. We both signed up and by the following April we were flying out to Sarajevo. It was such a wonderful experience both heartbreaking when you discover what the people endured and heartwarming to see how strong is the human resolve to get through such horrific trauma but still feel that life is worth living.

It was hard work seeing seven people a day Monday to

Friday for a fortnight and washing all the linen and towels each night ready for the clinic the next day. When we say clinic this is nothing like we are used to here. Treatment areas are in buildings with areas sectioned off with wire and curtains and in the outreach centres we set up wherever we could and often in buildings still bearing the scars of war. Nothing fancy but a much-needed service all the same. We learned phrases in Bosnian for, "Hello, please sit down, hurt, pain, leg, back, please turn over" but the language barrier didn't matter. We had two lovely ladies as interpreters, Nadiya and Enisa.

For my part, I'm sure my massages improved after the experience of treating people with emotional trauma and physical scars such as shrapnel in their bodies or amputations. I am more sensitive to clients' needs. Sometimes things went wrong with the equipment and at one of the outreach centres, Mel had to put her DIY skills to the test when a massage couch collapsed. Although we went in April once the weather warmed up the heat was searing to work in but the clients were amazing. Many of them are still refugees and don't have a lot in life but they would bring in presents, which was often food, to express their gratitude and I've never been hugged and kissed so much in my life.

It wasn't all work and no play. We did venture down the very steep hill from the flat into the centre of Sarajevo which is a beautiful city. There were some lovely eating places and the Old Town where traditional crafts are still made and sold and the walks amid beautiful scenery.

We took a tram to their Vrelo National Park and dipped our feet fleetingly into the stream of ice meltwater running down from the mountains. We also discovered Bosnian beer! I can tell you now that the hill back up to the flat was steep enough at the best of times but after a few bottles of that beer, it was damn near impossible.

PART III

Corporate Massage And What The Future Holds For Massage Therapy

7

Chapter 7: Step Inside

CORPORATE MASSAGE & HOW TO GET THROUGH THE DOOR

"I want to get into businesses, how do you do it?" is the question I get asked more than any about running the business. So many therapists want to take massage into businesses and my stock answer has always been it takes a long time which, to be honest, isn't helpful to anyone.

I've set out below the areas we explored which resulted in getting businesses on board where some were more successful than others.

Relevant Massage Training for Onsite Work

I remember noticing literature at the training school about a chair massage course which sparked my interest. My friend, Amanda[1], who also trained on the same massage course, was keen to do it too. Our training school didn't have any forthcoming dates but we found another college about a month or so later running a weekend course so we both booked on.

I have to say it wasn't really what I was expecting. There were no proper massage chairs, just normal wooden chairs, and the person receiving the massage sat on the chair the "wrong way round" if you know what I mean, so facing the back of the chair. They may have had a cushion to hold I cannot remember and then it was just a simple routine of massage movements over the back and shoulders. But hey presto! At the end of the weekend, we had a certificate to say we could do onsite massage–frightening!

I'm not saying all weekend courses are inferior and not worth doing but do be careful which course you choose. Check too that they are accredited by a professional association such as the Federation of Holistic Therapists or the Complementary Therapists Association otherwise you may struggle to obtain insurance cover.

Thankfully, most course providers do require you to have a minimum of Level 3 Holistic Massage so you have an understanding of the muscles you are working on and areas to avoid, pathology, and so on but I would be a little concerned about people with no experience attending one sunny Sunday afternoon and coming out with a piece of paper saying they can start doing onsite massage.

I wanted to pursue corporate work. Thankfully at a holistic fair in Birmingham, an onsite massage academy was showcasing the seated acupressure massage and with details of a course starting later that year close to where I lived, I booked on. It was an intense course and just felt right.

Luckily, I met a lady there fairly local to me and she ran an onsite massage business so after I completed the course I bought a massage chair and did some agency work for her. It was a good experience and I am grateful to her for giving me the opportunity.

Where Do You Find Your Client Companies?

Most of our clients have found us through searching the internet or our website or we have met them at networking events but there are other avenues to consider.

Through Volunteering

We have talked about the pros and cons of giving your time away for free but sometimes good things happen. My first corporate client came through a contact when I volunteered at our local hospice which is very well respected and well supported in the local community. They attend many networking events and told me about a local women's networking group that was holding an event at the County Cricket Club. They suggested I asked if I could take my massage chair along which I did. During the evening an exuberant enthusiastic lady bounded over wanting to try the massage. Afterward, she exclaimed she wanted this for her patients. It turns out she was a partner in a dentist practice which had a good reputation for putting their patients at ease and thought something like the massage to offer to them to calm their nerves would be a great idea.

I was over the moon.

That started a weekly visit to the dentist practice where one of the downstairs rooms wasn't used on a Tuesday so I set up the chair in there and I sat in the waiting room chatting to the patients awaiting their dental appointments asking if anyone wanted to have a back and shoulder or head massage while they were waiting.

I had agreed with the practice that I would charge a nominal amount for a 10-15-minute treatment and then give the practice a percentage of it. But my shyness and lack of persuasion skills prevented me from making a good go of it. I would sit there between 10 am and 4 pm and maybe only see a handful of people; sometimes, none at all. I did gain one elderly lady as a regular but that was all.

The practice manager was brilliant trying to think of different ways of letting patients know in advance that I would be there so that they would allow extra time but it wasn't a viable business operation.

I carried on convincing myself it was a good idea with thoughts such as, "I'm not that busy anyway so sitting at the dental practice all day on a Tuesday is okay." Or, "If I was busier I wouldn't do it."

In other words, I was making excuses for myself as to why I should continue sitting there all day for little return. In the end, the practice said they needed to use that downstairs room so it came to a natural end. In hindsight that may have been their polite way of saying it was a good idea to start with but hadn't worked!

Previous Workplaces And Existing Clients

Think about who you already know, your private clients, where do they work, is it something that would be of interest to their employers? What about friends and family, partners or spouses, would they have any business contacts? It helps to have a named contact and particularly if you can mention that someone from within that firm or someone one trusted by the firm has given you their details.

Where have you worked previously? Would they be interested in having you in one day a week or a month to provide the massage to your ex-colleagues? Mel had been working part-time at the local hospital trust but decided to leave to do therapies full time. She had already opened the door at the hospital offering the chair massage to colleagues on her day off and so when she left she carried this on at the various hospital sites.

I used to work in law firms and in my last full-time job I was also a member of the local branch of the Chartered Institute of Legal Executives. At one of their meetings, I was speaking with a legal executive and she said her firm used to have someone attend to do aromatherapy treatments. She gave me the name of the person I needed to contact in HR and we agreed I could use one of the meeting rooms and the staff members would pay individually. That was about seven years ago and eventually, the numbers increased so that we changed from monthly visits to fortnightly visits.

Agency Work

Agency work is one way of doing workplace massage as you do not have to find the clients yourself and you start building your experience of working in those environments. I would imagine most if not all can be found on the internet and many agencies work nationwide.

Sign up with as many as you can as work can be very ad hoc at times. I always say to anyone joining my team that I cannot guarantee regular work all the time. I have some therapists on the team where I have only been able to find one or two one-off assignments for them but others have landed regular fortnightly or monthly clients. I know many of the therapists I use also work for other agencies and I believe you can build up several working hours doing it this way.

The downside, of course, is that agency fees will never be as lucrative as having those clients in your own right but it is all good experience.

Business Parks

After eighteen months of working in the therapy room at the shop, it closed as the company went into liquidation. This forced my hand, I had a decision to make.

Do I try to find another therapy room to work from, do I set up at home, or do I do mobile massage?

I didn't particularly want to work from home. Clients I had amassed wanted me to stay in the city centre but rentals at hairdressers were extortionate, wanting a daily rate far in excess at that time than I was even making in a week.

A lady who ran a ladies-only gym did offer us an area

downstairs which was curtained off but it was very noisy with the gym being in an open plan area above us and in any case, she also went out of business very soon after. I decided to do mainly mobile massage for my private clients and felt this was telling me it was time to direct my focus towards corporate massage.

I needed to build my business back up again. I searched the internet and found a local business park where one of the buildings was a serviced office unit which means several businesses rent rooms in the one building, there is a serviced reception area and communal kitchen and bathrooms but otherwise, each level of the building would house different independent businesses.

Now, you may be thinking, that was probably expensive. This particular company however offered short-term lets of six months at a fixed rate which covered all expenses so you knew exactly how much was required each month. I decided to bite the bullet, set a budget, and signed up for an initial six months as I thought being there would at least give me a presence in the business arena and also I had a vision of all the independent businesses in the building flocking to our little office to have their massages during the working day. Did they heck, it was like pulling teeth getting anyone to move away from their desks and venture outside of their office doors.

We put our leaflets in the kitchen areas on each floor and reception told everyone about us. They all said it was a great idea but as soon as it came to parting with money and using the service there was a wall of silence. Very disheartening as Mel and I had worked out who would go in on which days to service the many clients we thought we would have.

The residents of the office building may not have been willing but all was not lost. One day I was standing in reception talking and could feel someone's eyes burning into my back. I turned around and a man was sitting on one of the chairs reading the wording on the back of my polo shirt which said "Bringing Massage 2U, De-stress and refresh in just 20 minutes" (that was a strapline thought up by Mel which I think is great and we still use in one form or another today) and my phone number. He asked if we only offered our service there as his head office was in a different place. I said we could go over to his head office and there and then he made an appointment. That was the start of a good working relationship that saw us attending their head office and satellite offices every month for a good few years.

Our first regular corporate client!

The sales team from the serviced office building were also supportive. We decided when we took on the rental that it would be a good idea to have a launch evening and they were happy for us to use one of the meeting rooms. We invited all the local businesses on the business park and anyone else we could think of and ran a business competition so that one of the businesses had a chance to win ten sessions of the seated acupressure massage at their office.

The business who won the ten sessions was a small IT company, just the type of business that would benefit from the massage as they are working at computers all day. Would you believe it? They didn't seem too enthusiastic apart from one of their employees and so his boss said he could have all ten sessions instead of the firm taking part. A little disappointing to say the least although I have to say that after the initial free sessions ended, this particular man did carry on with having paid sessions and at times managed to persuade some of his colleagues. I would attend monthly for a few years or more. Not very profitable from a business point of view, but it was only a mile and a half up the road from me so I kept it going.

Tracey Nash[2], a marketing lady I met through the first networking group I attended and who had suggested Bringing Massage 2u as the name of the business, used her contacts to advertise the launch. She also arranged for the local BBC radio station to send over a reporter on another day to do a live broadcast while she tried the massage. On the day, they had technical problems so it didn't go out live but broadcast later.

It was a young girl who came and while Mel was giving her a massage on the chair I was talking about the benefits but I remember one unhelpful thing she said when trying to describe what the massage chair looked like, she said it was like having your face stuck in a padded toilet seat. Great! That'll bring the punters in. I don't think we got any enquiries from that particular news item.

Cold Calling

The sales team also had another building in a nearby location and arranged for us to do some taster sessions. We set up in one of their meeting rooms and Mel and I took it in turns to do the massaging. I decided when Mel was massaging to take our leaflets round to other businesses on the business development. The only problem with this is most businesses now don't let you into the building until you talk to someone over the intercom. You try selling the benefits of your business and persuade someone to let you in when you are standing on the pavement outside and all you can hear is a crackly voice. It's not easy and to be honest this type of cold calling wasn't very successful apart from one place.

It was a local housing association where you could walk into the building and speak to someone on reception. I asked if there was anyone available to speak to from human resources and thankfully someone did come down to see me. I explained what we did and it was a case of being in the right place at the right time, as she said they had been talking about health and wellbeing and in particular about workplace massage but hadn't known where to begin looking. She took my details and said they would be in touch. True to her word, a little while later she contacted me to say that they were having a staff health and wellbeing day and did we want to attend to promote the massage.

Initially, that was another freebie but the good thing was that they also subscribed to a health cash plan company and their representative was also onsite that day. I had a chat with him and it turned out that they covered workplace massage under their policy. So, if we charged the individual member of staff for the massage, as long as we gave them a receipt, they could then reclaim the cost of the massage under the plan. Heaven! Everybody would gain from this, the housing association by providing the staff the time to have the massages, us because we would get paid and the staff because they would recoup the cost. Another regular client about to be added to the books.

Chamber Of Commerce

One of the other benefits of having taken the business let is that they put on our desk information about the local Chamber of Commerce. A representative came to see me to explain how they support local businesses.

There was a membership fee but as we were a small concern it wasn't too expensive and we could pay in instalments. It opened up a whole new world of networking for us and the staff were incredibly supportive. They even chose us to be on one of the banner photographs when they revamped their website, how cool is that?

We started attending breakfast and lunch meetings where we met other local businesses. As time passed, we also joined two other Chambers of Commerce when we expanded our team and I have to say they have been a great source of work for us.

Attending Networking Groups

Networking is always a good place to start but think about the people you need to speak with and which groups they are likely to attend. We have found that Women's Business Forums and HR Forums work for us as it is often HR advisors who are tasked with health and wellbeing policies. Find out who the speakers are at events too, if there is a speaker on health and wellbeing that would be a good event to go to as you would presume that at least some of the people there have booked on because of the subject matter and so you will be with like-minded people.

Some Chambers and businesses such as legal firms may also run their events for HR people tackling issues around employment and cover matters such as health and safety and wellbeing issues. These are the people you need to speak to. Some events will send out a delegate list before the meeting, scour this to see who else will be there and pinpoint those who work in places that may be of interest to you.

Other people in the wellbeing sector are also good contacts. I said earlier about other health professionals such as physios or osteopaths, talk to them to see if there could be a connection there to work together.

The main thing is to show up at as many meetings as you can, some will be free, others will have a cost so your budget will be a factor but get yourself known. Remember what we said about networking and not going to meetings purely looking to make a sale but to get to know others, get to know their businesses, and have conversations not only about work but other things too, get to know people as people rather than just the potential gateway into a business. This is where you will need to find out which meetings work for you. Some are very structured and may not allow enough time for general networking, others are more laid back, it depends on what works for you.

Something I feel didn't help me initially is that I wasn't aware of anyone else locally who was doing corporate massage. No-one else at networking events does what I do and so there was no competition.

How can that be bad? Well, it is bad if you are generally a pretty laid back sort of person, a non-go-getter if that is a phrase, an introvert by nature, because if there is no urgency then why create some? If there had been another business trying to get into the firms I wanted and was vying for their business, it would have been the 2,000 volts up my backside that I needed to make sure I got in there first!

But apart from a few years in when another therapist did appear on the scene for a while, I had that market all to myself. The good side to it as I have mentioned before is that because what we were doing is different from most businesses in the room, we are memorable.

Business Expos

I believe our best platform for creating interest in what we do is local business expos. Some of them are run by the Chambers of Commerce, others are local firms or event organisers who run them. We turn up with our massage chair, set up the stand with our banners and literature, have at least two people to man the stand, and offer complimentary 5-10 minute seated massages. It goes down a storm every time. We are always being told we must be one of the busiest stands there as once you get someone on the chair, it spikes curiosity, and other people, attendees, and other stand holders will come over for their 10 minutes of relaxation.

More often than not towards the end of the expo when everyone is dismantling their stands we will still be massaging and having to turn people away. Okay, who doesn't like a free massage? But, it brings people over and this is why we always have at least two people, so one can be doing the massaging and the other person can talk to the queue of people waiting for their massage about what we do. I would say 99.9% of the time we will always get at least one job from those expos and plenty of enquiries to follow up.

You will have a ton of business cards by the end of the day (always collect a business card or contact information from everyone having a massage as well as those who just visit your stand). Don't just stash them away and think you'll look at those later, make sure you follow up on every one of them. There is no point being at an expo all day if you don't follow up on the leads.

I always write a note on each card to remind me who that person was because at the end of the day you will not remember everyone you spoke to. For example, if someone was interested in obtaining a quote, I would ask them how many employees they have and where they are based and write that on the card so I can provide a bespoke quotation.

When we turn up at expos and set up our stand people come over to tell us they hoped we would be there. We also use social media before the event to advertise the fact that we will be there to create conversations and a buzz before the event even takes place.

I believe these events are worth the investment. It allows you to walk around the other stands and talk to people face to face. It is much easier to explain to someone what you do by talking to them rather than relying on emails. People are there to talk, the environment lends itself to you having the opportunity to find out about other businesses and talk to them about yours in a friendly and relaxed manner.

Using Social Media

Another avenue for "warm" contact rather than cold calling is by using platforms such as LinkedIn. At first, LinkedIn was seen more of a job-seeking site but it has certainly turned into more than that in recent years and we now use it more than ever for posting blogs and articles and also to comment on other people's posts. If you engage with other firms, particularly your clients, and also those you would like to work with, it is a good place to be seen.

People are notified if anyone comments or likes posts and so your name will be in front of them. You could send them a message and say that you enjoyed reading their post and would like to connect with them which starts a conversation. You decide whether to take it further from there with a scheduled phone call. I would keep it friendly and only if you honestly were interested in what they were posting. No-one likes to be spammed by someone asking for a connection and then immediately selling to them. It's the same principle as with face to face networking build up a relationship and get to know them.

This is where social media is an important part of networking and getting introductions to firms. It does take up a lot of time but it is worth putting in the effort.

Twitter gets conversations started and again is a good platform to retweet other people's posts and comment on them and get talking. We also use it for saying where we are working or posting blogs with a call to action to contact us if you would like to know more about what we do.

Even better if you can post your own blogs and ideas for other people to comment on. That may sound a bit scary and I must admit I shied away from doing so for quite some time but it's another way of people getting to know you and as they say you never know who those people know. If they retweet, your post will be seen by many more people than you will ever know.

Website

Since we revamped our website the last time, I have to say we do get quite a few enquiries through the contact page from all different areas of the country. It just proves that the money spent working with people who know what needs to be done "behind the pages" to make sure the site is visible has paid for itself. The website, networking, and attending expos are our most successful routes to attracting clients.

Who Pays?

Another common question is: who pays for the service? Is it the employer, the employee or is there a subsidised scheme? We have come across all three with our clients but the overall majority is where the employer pays and to be honest if they are really serious about looking after their employees' health and wellbeing, they ought to be looking at it as a return on investment. If staff feel valued and happy this leads to engaged and motivated teams. Don't get me started on that though, that is a whole topic in its own right!

The other advantage where the employer pays is that you can agree on an hourly rate or a half/full day rate depending on how many people you are seeing. If you are going to be somewhere for a half or full-day remember to factor in some breaks as it is a tiring day doing short sessions one after the other.

One of the local NHS Trusts was running a scheme for nine months where they offered staff various health and wellbeing activities at subsidised rates and the workplace massage was one of them. The staff paid half the fee and we invoiced the Trust for the other half. Needless to say, the appointments slots were always fully booked and we attended every week. After the scheme finished we carried on offering the sessions but numbers dropped like a stone. The staff viewed it as the price has doubled rather than accepting that they had only paid half the normal rate. We dropped the sessions down to once a month and gradually over time the numbers started to increase again but it took ages to recover. So, just be careful with subsidised schemes and make sure the clients know they are only paying a proportion of the normal rate.

We do have a few clients where the employer is happy for the staff to take the time to have a massage but they expect the individuals to pay so you rely on headcount. That's okay if everyone who has booked turns up but that's not always the case. Some sessions are fine, others you can be waiting around for hours and only a handful arrive for the appointments. This is a bugbear and why where possible it is better if the employer pays.

I have been guilty in many cases over the years of plugging away at sites where the individuals pay but where the numbers aren't great. You do have to make a business decision in the end as to whether they are worth keeping on.

It's not all doom and gloom: there is one client company I attend where the individuals pay and for ages, it didn't make business sense to carry on going but over time and with a new influx of employees it gradually built up again and is now profitable.

How Can I Compete With The Larger Onsite Massage Businesses?

I wouldn't worry about that at all. I know it's something therapists think about but honestly, it depends on the clients you are after and most of our clients are what I would class as small to medium-sized enterprises. Occasionally, we provide our services to larger national companies but they tend to be for once or twice yearly wellbeing events rather than regular sessions. A misconception we hear at networking events is that we only go to large corporations as they are the ones who can afford it. This is nonsense as the service we provide is not expensive but reaps huge benefits and it is often the smaller local companies who are responsive to what we do and can make the decisions without having to plough through loads of red tape.

Think about how many people you could see in a day, maybe around 15 – 20 for seated massage sessions? Not everyone in a business will take up the massage, whether that is because not everyone is on-site every day, they may be out at meetings, or the firm decides on a limited number of sessions and there will always be people who just don't want a massage. A business with say 60-70 people might book a day with you to see 15-20 members of staff. That's a pretty decent-sized firm and one that you are very likely to meet at local networking events. It doesn't matter that it is just you on your own, you don't have to have a large team behind you.

But What If You Do Want to Grow the Business?

Do you know when something is so blindingly obvious you just can't see it? The recruitment firm who had been with us right from the start expanded tremendously opening several new offices, and as the original offices were used to having our services the new ones would want the same. The only issue was that the new offices were outside of what would be a reasonable commute for me. So what to do?

I told them to leave it with me and I'll see if I can find a therapist in those areas. Well, the first two were okay, I found a therapist through the support group. The next office to open was even further afield so I scoured the professional associations' directories of therapists to find someone in that area. I did find a therapist, had a meeting with her and she came on board. Everything was good.

After this new set up for the recruitment company had been going for a while I suddenly had a lightbulb moment. It dawned on me if I could find therapists for the recruitment company then I could find therapists for anyone outside the area.

I remember only a year previously receiving an email from a company in the North of England which was way out of my area asking if we did the workplace massage up there and I replied by saying no, sorry. That would not happen now, I would say yes, of course, in the first instance and then if I didn't have anyone, I would source someone. That is how the business started to expand, especially across the Midlands which is where we were known, and then further afield. I do put pressure on myself by doing it this way: on occasion I have found it more difficult than anticipated to find therapists in some areas until the eleventh hour, but only twice have I had to travel a huge distance to cover a job because I couldn't find anyone to cover it.

This was my first experience of realising I had been a little insular in my thinking and just jogging along, content with the clients I had. In itself, there is nothing wrong with that if my ambition was to stay small and local (it would be much less hassle if it had stayed like that). However, my idea was to grow the business and so I had to change my way of thinking.

I remember when we had only been operating for a year or so, we were asked by the local NHS Trust if we would take our chairs to offer massages on their stand at a health and wellbeing expo. That in itself was great fun to do and probably the first time we had offered the service of being on someone else's stand to entice people over. We also met another lady who had her stand and was offering massages. She ran an onsite massage business and talking to her I remember her saying that offering the service on a national level is a whole different ballgame to keeping it local and she was right.

Finding Therapists to Join the Team

Sourcing therapists is based on trust as I cannot physically get to see everyone depending on where in the country they are. I do try to have a telephone conversation with them though as I think you can get a feel for someone's personality by having a chat and asking them about their experience, why they set up doing massage, and what they enjoy about it. As we have all got used to doing video calls during the Coronavirus lockdown I think a Zoom or Skype call may be on the cards from now on.

The team has grown by putting out requests on various platforms to say I have a job coming up in a particular area and inviting therapists to contact me if they are interested. I use the Forums for Employment Opportunities on professional association websites, posts in Facebook Groups for mobile massage therapists and also on training school websites, and Facebook pages. More often than not I receive replies from more therapists than I need so I ask those who I cannot offer the job to if I have their permission to keep hold of their details for future work. The answer is usually yes and I now have a bank of other therapists ready if more work comes up in that area.

I also look to the "Find A Therapist" directories on professional association websites and online business directories and contact people individually. This is where I put out my plea to ensure you have at least a phone number but preferably an email address as well with your details as it is so frustrating to know your name but no idea how to contact you. If you have a website please also make sure that information is listed too, it makes my life so much easier and stops me from wasting your time if you don't do the therapies I'm looking for. Hand on heart so far, I have only been let down a couple of times, which is still two too many but not bad odds for a decade of trading.

A couple of the therapists who are on our team also do a similar thing running their agencies and sometimes if they are struggling to find someone for a particular job, I will suggest some therapists on our team if they are in that area. It also works the other way if I am struggling they will try to find therapists for me. Technically, we compete with each other but I have always been a firm believer that there is enough work out there for everyone so why not help each other out? You will also find that therapists on the team refer other therapists to you and so that has also helped to grow the team. From just the two of us at the beginning, we now have a bank of over 100 therapists.

Just one last point on growing a team: I said at the beginning of the chapter about training schools offering weekend courses for seated massage and that the quality of some leave much to be desired, whereas others offer good quality training. If you have a client company looking to have the workplace massage covered by a health cash plan, some of those cash plans only accept named accredited courses. So if your qualification isn't covered by one of those accredited courses the employees will not be able to claim back their money.

There are certain training providers I trust implicitly and if, when looking for a therapist, I see that they have trained with one of those schools, I know I can trust them to do a good job.

Who Do You Trust?

In addition to expos, networking is the next best platform for us and certainly in our geographical area, we are well-known and recognised. It's a case of plodding away, turning up at events, keep the conversation going on social media, and get yourself known.

One of the highlights for me happened a few years ago at a social event but was attended by several local business people. Someone I had met a few times at networking but did not know particularly well said to me during a conversation that I was known as the go-to person for anything health and wellbeing. I cannot tell you how that boosted my confidence (and my ego of course)—I was floating on air. I was also asked recently if I would write an article for one of the Chambers of Commerce business magazine about developing a health and wellbeing strategy in the workplace. I could never have imagined doing that even a few years ago so again, the fact that they had thought to ask me felt like an incredible privilege.

We've been around long enough now for people to trust us, to trust we know what we are doing. We love what we do and we are happy to help other businesses too.

8

Chapter 8: Then Everything Stopped

WHERE DO WE GO FROM HERE?

It's March 2020 and all massage therapy has to stop due to the Government lockdown imposed to lessen the blow of Coronavirus on the overstretched NHS.

At first, I imagined it would be for just a few weeks. I still set the alarm for silly-o'clock in the morning and worked frantically on all the non-appointment work that gets left behind when you're racing around seeing clients. It felt good because I had often thought, "Why can't everything stop for a while so I can catch up?" I now had my opportunity—but then the realisation set in that it was going to be a long haul.

As I'm writing this, close-contact services, which include massage, have been given the green light to proceed again with many restrictions and enhanced hygiene measures. We must wear face masks and visors but at least many therapists are back working now in their private practices.

It highlighted how financially vulnerable we are in our profession: we were one of the last to be advised we could recommence work. It's understandable in many ways considering the close physical contact we have with our clients, but a heavy burden all the same.

We should take this experience to think about how we may

plan to create a financial buffer should anything like the pandemic happen in the future. Sadly, some great therapists have been lost along the way as the financial losses were too much to bear and there was too much uncertainty—but there have to be some positives to emerge.

Personally, although the zero income was a pain in the backside, like many people it has given me time to reflect on business, life, the Universe, and in some ways I have found having the time to think has led me to believe we can turn the business around to cater for the new way of doing things. Most of our clients are businesses and many of those have furloughed staff or had others working from home. Some are slowly going back to the office but it may be some time before new routines are established. We started looking at what could be offered online and the therapists on the team are a talented bunch. It soon became apparent that some could offer online sessions of yoga, pilates, nutrition workshops, laughter workshops and mindfulness, meditation, Qi Gong, and dance therapy.

Even if some businesses retain working from home as part of its new of working there will be times when teams need to get together so we are looking at what can be provided to ensure those working from home do not feel isolated and still feel part of the team as well as activities for team building days. I also believe coaching and counselling will become important to address mental health issues which may become apparent in the aftermath of the pandemic.

I have also been taking part in video networking meetings and was asked to be a speaker for one of them talking about the ergonomics of setting up your workspace at home, so there are always opportunities there to be visible and let people know you are still in business.

We also realised that if employees are working remotely they may like to have private massage treatments at home or a salon or clinic so we emailed offering this service and to check with us if we had a therapist in their area. This way, the clients know we are still here and looking after them and it also gives the therapists on the team the chance to gain some private work.

It's been great to have time to practice what we preach about self-care. I have incorporated more exercise into my days and formed new habits to ensure I keep on the move as much as possible. I'm sure my eating has improved too because I'm not racing around in the car from one place to another and just grabbing food on the way (which inevitably includes chocolate). As another therapist told me, she feels re-energised.

It is also evident that our clients are still out there, they haven't gone away and they are desperate for our services. This is a good time to review your vision and business plan as you may not be able to see so many clients in one day as extra time is required for enhanced hygiene procedures and ventilation of rooms. It may be that from now on we all work in different ways but there is always going to be a need for us and now is the time to make sure we return to it but on our terms.

Remember the nice things people say about you, here are a couple of quotes from therapists on my team which shows what a lovely caring lot we are!

"The most important thing for me to be a good therapist is to listen to the client and suit the massage to his needs. During the 10 years of my practice in various places, I have often met with therapists who performed the same movements on each client. You have to open your heart and mind and find what is needed at the moment, not to do everything we've learned at school."

"Being a therapist is a great vocation, not just a job, to make a success of it you need to immerse yourself in it, keep it vital and new, don't get complacent or stale, be interested in learning and taking yourself on a journey, take hold of the subjects within it that interest you the most, you will naturally succeed in something you enjoy, and clients will be drawn to that."

"You occasionally come across someone who is quite anxious about the whole idea of massage, it then helps to have a little fun and relax the clients, working only within their limits and not belittling yourself that you couldn't provide the full massage you had expected to.

Providing the massage they need and reading them, their needs, and responses are much more important than anything you think you know about what they need. Flexibility and adapting to each individual is so important. The sense of humour and being laid back also helps with the odd client who tries to take their clothes off for a seated massage or who decide to lay stark naked and uncovered on your couch when you've told them to leave pants on!"

Be positive, be confident, value what you do, and above all enjoy it.

9

Chapter 9: Can You Remember Everything You've Read?

CHAPTER HIGHLIGHTS

I have highlighted here the main areas of focus from each Chapter. This isn't a textbook so it is not in the form of exercises, but I hope it gives you food for thought and a useful reference as to what has been covered.

Chapter 1: Why Are You Doing This?

- What is your Why?
- Write down 5 core values, things that are important to you in work and life generally.
- Does your current work/life reflect those values, if not, list improvements you can make (small changes can go a long way).
- Determine your priorities.
- Create a vision of what your ideal business looks like.
- Get that vision board started either as an actual board or as saved documents, pictures, sayings in a folder on the computer.
- Create the whole picture—work and lifestyle.

- Create a business plan.
- Work out sensibly how many clients you can see which also allows you non-appointment time and a life outside of work.
- How much do you want to earn? How does that relate to the numbers of clients you can see in a week?
- Do you have other income streams i.e. sales of essential oils, other products, teaching?
- Incorporate downtime into your business plan, make appointments with yourself to have time away from work.

Chapter 2: Who Are You Looking For?

Who is your ideal client?

Create a description of your ideal client (your client avatar):

- Who are they, age, gender, lifestyle, specific issues e.g. sports injuries, bad posture, stuck at a computer all day, looking after a young family
- What is their pain? What do they struggle with, physically, emotionally, practically?
- How can your massage/other therapy help them—describe how they will feel.

How to get your message across:

- Remember your ideal client and that you are talking to them.
- Concentrate on the specific benefits and how it will make your client feel.
- Think about the layout of a brochure and what information you would include.

- What is the story which will encourage your client to make an appointment?

Chapter 3: Branding and Marketing

The values you wrote down as being important to you form part of your brand. With that in mind:

- How would you describe your business to someone who doesn't know you?
- How are your values reflected in your business?

Standing out from everyone else:

- Avoid stock images and templated designs as far as possible for marketing literature. Do you know someone who could take some good quality photographs for you?
- Research designs, logos, and colours that you like and collect examples.

Would professional help be useful to design something for you which you can use consistently in everything you do? Obtain quotations from design and print/graphic design/web design businesses.

Do you have a website?

- Are you happy with it or could you do with some professional help? If so, as above ask for quotes for designing a website too.
- Meet with the potential designers to get a feel for the way they work and if they are on the same wavelength to you as cost should not be the only consideration. They need to understand your message.

How well do you use social media to promote your brand? Facebook Page:

- Set up a business page if you have not done so already
- Work out a schedule of postings e.g. Friday Feelgood Tips or availability of appointments or articles on the benefits of reflexology, Indian head massage, holistic massage, or whatever you specialise in but do it consistently so that people look out for your new posts.

Instagram, Twitter, LinkedIn, YouTube channel:

- Do you have current profiles? With LinkedIn especially, a 100% completed profile will aid your visibility.
- Make time in your diary as appointments to spend time preparing articles or posts or photographs for these platforms.
- Comment on other people's posts to show interest.
- Investigate the costs of hiring someone to assist you with this.

Start writing blogs:

- What do you know about e.g. the benefits of the different therapies you practice?
- Comments on relevant articles you have read.
- Write about events you will be/have attended and what you did there.
- Write blogs in such a way that your personality shines through (they don't have to be deadly serious).
- As soon as you think of an idea of what you can

write about, write it down, build up a bank of ideas.

Promoting your brand: where do your ideal clients go? Where will you find them?

Local Community Groups: investigate local groups and if they hold fundraising events such as ladies' pamper evenings where you can take your massage couch/chair and offer mini treatments for a fee.

Sports Clubs:

- Are you ideal clients likely to be members of local sports clubs or gyms?
- Investigate if there are opportunities for you to work onsite or in collaboration with them.
- Consider volunteering at local events such as 10k runs.

Online Directories:

- Search the internet for free directories and prepare a listing remembering your message and how to get that across in a short description.
- Search for paid sites and weigh up the cost with the likely return of enquiries.
- Add your details to "Find a Therapist" pages on Professional Association' websites.

Advertising:

- Look for local community pages online, some offer free listings rather than paid advertising.
- Local community brochures will often allow you to have an editorial piece if you also pay for a quarter or half page advert.

- Facebook Ads – I would suggest taking advice from a marketing/social media expert as to how to use these to your best advantage.
- Think about your ideal client and whether your advert will reach them i.e. is the magazine/brochure/online platform one that they will see.

Corporate video:

- Investigate professional video companies even if you think you may not be able to afford it initially.
- Think about doing your own short videos to upload to your Facebook Page and other online platforms.
- These could be tips and advice relating to a blog you have posted.
- It could just be a relaxed "Hi, how is everyone feeling today?" type post.
- Feeling brave? Do a Facebook Live!

Chapter 4: You Mean I Have To Talk To People

Networking Groups: search the internet for networking groups in your area. See if they have an online presence too as you may be able to glean information from their website as to how they structure their meetings if there are any fees involved and where they meet.

Which of these do you think would work for you?

- Business Groups with a structured agenda who meet early in the morning.
- Those who are not quite so structured but still have a 40/60 second pitch.

- Breakfast meetings, mid-morning or lunch meetings, early evening after work.
- Business Women's Networking Forums.
- Meetings run by the local Chamber of Commerce.
- Social meetings without the 40/60 second pitch
- Local community group meetings.

Are you better talking to people first thing in the morning or would lunchtimes or early evening groups work better for you? Work on that 40/60 second pitch and have a few that you learn off by heart to dampen those nerves.

- Prepare before a meeting what you are going to say.
- Have several pitches depending on the "audience" at the group.
- Be specific about the referrals you're looking for.
- Tell a story to get your message across.
- Smile!

Look into your local Chambers of Commerce as they are a good support network as well as attending their events.

Remember it is always about conversations, you do not need to be a salesperson.

Speaking Slots:

- Be brave and put yourself forward for a speaking slot.
- Practice by video on your phone to build your confidence.
- Prepare a few so that you are ready and willing!

Chapter 5: Stop Being So Nice!

Value what you do. List all the things you do currently where you give your time for free and how it makes you feel. For example:

- Giving clients more than their allotted time.
- Not charging a decent rate for treatments.
- Giving discounts as you are being pressurised by the client to do so.
- Giving your time for free at events.

What is stopping you from making a change?

If this was someone else's business and you were the business advisor, what would you say?

When was the last time you increased your prices?

Have your expenses increased over that time?

How can you get value from promotional events?

Have you put a cancellation policy in place? Think about doing this and making your clients aware of it.

Chapter 6: Self Care

When was the last time you had a massage or any form of complementary therapy?

- Form a habit of making regular appointments to have treatments/downtime.
- Book on to CPD courses to help you improve your techniques to lessen the strain on your body.

Time management:

- Are you allowing sufficient time for the non-appointment work?

- Are there aspects of your business you could outsource such as administration or accounts?
- Reflect on your vision and business plan. Are you squeezing in too many clients in a day or week?

Join online support groups or look to create a local support group with therapists in your area.

Make time to practice some mindfulness if it is only 10 minutes a day to just stop. Sit quietly, do whatever works for you but switch off and relax. You owe it to yourself.

Chapter 7: Specifically Corporate

Where are your potential corporate clients to be found?

- Do you still have a daytime job as well as your therapies? If so, is there an opportunity there?
- Friends, relatives, where do they work, could they obtain a contact name of someone in HR?
- Where do your private clients work? Could they give you a contact name at their places of work?
- Attend networking events.
- Exhibit at trade shows.
- Join the local Chamber of Commerce for business support and a network of member businesses.
- Use social media platforms such as LinkedIn and start posting and commenting on other posts to get yourself noticed.

Consider who would be your ideal corporate client:

- What size of firm?
- What sector e.g. IT, office-based, manufacturing?
- Location?

- Is it just you or will you be working with other therapists?
- Consider doing agency work for other onsite massage companies and sign up to several for more work opportunities.

Do you want to build a team and create your own onsite agency?

- If so, will you stay local or offer your service nationwide?
- Consider the practicalities of sourcing your therapists.

Chapter 8: After the Pandemic

Think about revisiting your business plan: the Coronavirus guidelines issued by the Government may have affected the number of clients you can see in a day.

Are you able to put in place financial planning to help should we be thrown into another pandemic that would prevent you from working?

Can you offer services online such as talking therapies, yoga, mindfulness?

- Think about how you would offer these i.e. live video or pre-recorded sessions.
- If pre-recorded will these be professionally filmed to ensure good quality?
- How will you charge for these sessions?

10

Chapter 10: What Has Massage Ever Done For Me?

Isn't it great? Overall I mean, running your own massage business. I would sum up my feelings as fun and freedom and it started me thinking about the question: what has massage ever done for me? In fact, that was my working title for the book for ages. I've achieved and experienced more than I would have done if I was still working in an office doing a job I had fallen out of love with.

Being a massage therapist has given me:

- The freedom to be my own boss, prove to myself I can run a successful business and love doing it rather than dreading the alarm going off on a Monday morning.
- The opportunity practically every day to make people happy and feel better.
- The chance to meet so many people from all walks of life and listen to their stories—people I would never have come across if I was still working in an office.
- The privilege to do some volunteering in a foreign country meet extraordinary people and walk on

fire in the process (to raise money to go over to Bosnia).

- The platform to meet so many people through networking who over time have become really good friends.
- Oodles of fun along the way.
- A win in a business raffle draw to have an aerobatic flying lesson in a yellow peril bi-plane which was nerve-racking (those words "you are in control") exhilarating and calming all at the same time. I could never have imagined before doing loop-the-loop, barrel rolls, or hanging upside down by some straps, or flying a plane.
- An increase in my confidence and feelings of self-worth through building up the business and lessons I have learned from others and mentors along the way.
- An amazing chance to meet my idol, Eddie Izzard. Okay, this link is a little tenuous. I was asked by the local newspaper, as a local business person, to list ten things I want to do before I die. Head and shoulders above everything else at number one was to meet Eddie Izzard. I have always loved his comedy and I admire his sheer self-belief that you can achieve anything you want. A few years later, my friend Tracy, a fellow Eddie fan, tipped me off that he would be in the marketplace later that day on the Labour Party election campaign trail. Whoa! What was the first thing I said to him? "We're wearing the same colour lipstick!" It made him smile, we had a selfie and there you go, my top wish, one I never thought I would realise, had just come true. After that, I felt as if I too, could achieve anything.
- The guts to stand up in front of a room of people

and give a presentation I have written. I still go red, my voice still waivers, but I do it.
- A boost to my ego by being asked to write an article for a Chamber of Commerce business magazine.
- Huge satisfaction and pride in providing work for other therapists through building up the corporate agency work and a warm glowing feeling when I read feedback from the therapists that they like working for me. Thank you!
- The inspiration to rediscover my love of writing in the form of blogs, articles, and of course, this book.
- The freedom to take control of my life and to make the most of it.

What does massage mean to you? Write it down and pin it to that Vision Board!

Acknowledgements: I could not have done this without you

1. To my partner, Derek Larkin, despite being the most awful case study for my training, who has supported me over the years as I built up the business and not least for feeding me.
2. To the therapists I have met along the way, I have learned so much from you. In particular to Mel Harris who is as mad as a hatter. I enjoyed our time working and staying over in Liverpool. For that very cold, windy weekend at the Sunshine Festival staying in your camper van and waking up to find our gazebo would have been miles away if we hadn't tied it to the security fencing. For our two trips to Bosnia and sharing the experiences of meeting amazing people, a vibrant city, and not forgetting the beer.
3. To my friend Amanda Miguel-Lopez, we met on that first massage course and have remained friends ever since. You are the epitome of what business acumen means together with sheer determination and hard work to make your dream

of owning a spa a reality. You are also the only person I have ever allowed to wax my legs.

4. To all those therapists who turned up at my house for that first meeting of what became the Be Inspired group, thanks for the support, it meant so much.
5. To Alex Browning for your enthusiasm and never ending knowledge of essential oils.
6. To the Power Group ladies: Tracy Reck, Jane Brook, Fay Hildred, Jan Gill and Helen Davies for your inspiration and straight talking when I ummed and aah'd over difficult or downright daft decisions.
7. To Louise Blunt, my business mentor, whose straight talking no-nonsense experience strengthened my confidence and pointed me in the right direction to grow the business and to stop being so nice!
8. To Donna Thomas of TEACH Therapy for your wonderful CPD courses and for Darien Pritchard and Joanne Perkins for their brilliant teaching.
9. To Chantall Herbert for being so enthusiastic, smiley, supportive and keeping me on track, for all the networking you do, the conversations you have which bring in more and more clients.
10. To Launa Brooks for eking out of me awkward things I wouldn't normally talk about and being my social secretary to get me away from work.
11. To Vicky Fraser for giving me the oomph to write this book in the first place. I stalked you for a few years before taking the plunge.
12. To Spaghetti Agency, Jo and Todd, for the immense value you give to your clients. You are both incredible (I still have the Lego cowboy).
13. To Julie King Photography for the great photos on

our website and making it fun even though I am one of those people who hates having their photo taken.

14. To iD Creative Design, Jane and Nick for your inspiration and ideas.
15. To Tracy and Emma Reck personal trainers for keeping me in check with my fitness and pushing me to levels I never thought I would be able to do —miss you both.
16. All the lovely team at Hands On At Work: too many of you now to mention individually but you all do such a fantastic job and you make the business what it is.
17. To all the therapists who kindly sent me your experiences of working as massage therapists and which I have used in this book. In particular to Ewa Zielecka-Koziol, Debbie Foster, Sophie Taylor, and Heather Smith for allowing me to quote you.

Don't Leave Me This Way...

Now that you've almost finished reading this book, I would hate this to be the end of our relationship, so please stay in touch.

These are my social media links; I would love to connect with you:

Facebook:
www.facebook.com/handsonatwork.co.uk
Twitter:
www.twitter.com/HandsOnAtWork
LinkedIn personal:
www.linkedin.com/in/handsonatwork
LinkedIn company page:
www.linkedin.com/company/hands-on-at-work
Instagram:
www.instagram.com/handsonatwork
Website:
www.handsonatwork.co.uk
Email address:
info@handsonatwork.co.uk

I am always on the lookout for massage therapists to join the Hands On At Work team—in particular those trained in seated acupressure massage. We work across the United Kingdom so location is not a problem.

I would love to hear from you if you practice other complementary therapies too as business clients are looking for a range of wellbeing services onsite and online.

Drop me an email at info@handsonatwork.co.uk and we'll arrange to have a chat.

Finally, a request from me to you.

If you have purchased this book from an online store and they have a review section, would you leave a review? Or post some feedback on any of the social media links above.

Thank you!

Notes

1. Chapter 1: Why Are You Doing This?

1. Rob Holcroft: www.super-humans.com

2. Chapter 2: Who Are You Looking For?

1. https://www.gov.uk/government/publications/guide-to-the-general-data-protection-regulation
2. Natalie Bagnall of Bodycares https://bodycares.co.uk

3. Chapter 3: Identify Yourself and Shout About It

1. Jane Anson: www.idcreativedesign.co.uk
2. Chantall Herbert of Buzz Development.
3. Spaghetti Agency: www.spaghettiagency.co.uk
4. www.embodyforyou.com
5. www.ctha.com
6. www.fht.org.uk/findatherapist
7. www.therapy-directory.org.uk
8. www.naturaltherapypages.co.uk
9. Mick Foley of One Minute Wonder Video Production and DroneServices: www.oneminutewonders.co.uk

4. Chapter 4: You Mean I Have To Talk To People?

1. www.britishchambers.org.uk/page/join-a-chamber

6. Chapter 6: Who Looks After You?

1. Darien Pritchard: www.dynamicmassage.co.uk and tutor at TEACH Therapy: www.teachtherapy.co.uk
2. Gary Smith at Faultless Bookkeeping: Gary Smith www.faultlessbookkeeping.co.uk
3. www.healinghandsnetwork.org.uk

7. Chapter 7: Step Inside

1. Amanda Miguel-Lopez of Serene Sanctuary: www.serene-sanctuary.com
2. Tracey Nash of Nash Marketing and Secretarial Services: www.nash-marketing.co.uk

About the Author

Taking that massage course was the best career decision I ever made. When I was a child I never wanted to do what everyone else was doing. I remember friends taking ballroom dancing lessons or joining the Brownies and thinking "I don't want anyone telling me what to do in my spare time!" (I was all of seven years old.)

It was the same at school when it came to career advice. I had no idea what I wanted to do but I knew I didn't want to work in an office. I wanted to do something different from my friends who were applying for jobs in banks.

For the first 20 years, all I did was work in offices (how the years roll on when you're not looking) so when the midlife crisis kicked in it was definitely time to break out.

I gave in my notice without knowing what I was going to do and flew off to Mexico for a couple of weeks on my own supposedly to "clear my head."

That was never going to work.

I vaguely remember declaring 2004 was the year I would try out new things. Upon my return, a friend had arranged for us both to attend a Royal Yachting Association Competent Crew course in Southampton (thanks Pauline). I have never visited the Isle of Wight so many times. It was the longest five days of my life, living in close quarters with people I didn't know, sitting at strange angles within inches of the water, freezing cold much of the time, tying weird knots in ropes, and being so tired the one night neither of us had the energy to take off our wellies before crawling into our beds. I did say the next time I set foot on a yacht I would be sipping cocktails, not taking the helm.

I'm pretty sure that was also the year I won a raffle prize with the choice of having a massage or dumper truck driving: guess which one I chose? That was a pretty cold November evening in Northumberland in a one-ton truck getting stuck in the mud.

The next couple of years saw me doing some locum work, delivering Yellow Pages (when they were huge heavy directories), and Christmas relief work at the local Royal Mail sorting office. I enjoyed the camaraderie even though the work was repetitive. I reached a point where I could tell you the postcode of any town in the UK and I also found out where Santa Claus actually lives (but I'm not telling you).

I also did a plastering course thinking I could set myself up as a handywoman. It was great fun, so messy. The tutor said he ought to weigh me when I arrive in the morning and then again as I leave and charge me for the amount of plaster I was "wearing".

When I'm not working I love to listen to very loud music, and I'm especially partial to a wailing guitar. I love to dance (belly dancing was a favourite). Eddie Izzard is my inspiration. And I love doting on my chickens.

I suppose I could say that massage saved me from being a belly dancing plasterer, who would rather be on terra firma or in the air than on the water, and who may well have set off in her dumper truck to visit Father Christmas.

facebook.com/handsonatwork.co.uk

twitter.com/HandsOnAtWork

instagram.com/handsonatwork

linkedin.com/in/handsonatwork